Amos

Prophet of Social Justice

AMOS
PROPHET OF SOCIAL JUSTICE

by Page H. Kelley

*CONTEMPORARY
DISCUSSION SERIES*

Baker Book House
Grand Rapids, Michigan

To
Professor James Leo Green
who first taught me to appreciate
the prophets of Israel

Preface

When Amos left his flocks in the hills of Judah and headed northward into Israel, a new day had arrived in the history of God's dealings with his people. Amos was not the first prophet in Israel, for even Abraham and Moses bore this title, but he was the first prophet of his kind. He was the first in a succession of men raised up by God to interpret to Israel the crises in her history and to call her to repentance.

While Amos is sometimes described as a "writing prophet," it must never be forgotten that he was first and foremost a preacher. His messages were delivered orally in towns and cities throughout the Northern Kingdom. The nine short chapters in the Book of Amos probably contain only a fraction of what the great prophet had to say. They contain enough, however, to let us know that he was a fearless man with an overpowering sense of divine call, a man who proclaimed the word of God without ever adapting it to the desires of his listeners.

The present Book of Amos is composed of brief utterances or messages of the prophet, together with a few brief biographical notes. We can be grateful to the faithful remnant in Israel that cherished and preserved these words and handed them down to future generations.

An effort has been made to examine each of these brief messages in some detail. No attempt has been made to weld these separate messages together into a unity, except where the context seemed to demand it. If this gives a disjointed character to the discussion guides, the author sees no legitimate way to avoid this since the disjointedness is inherent in the text of Amos itself.

These discussion guides have been prepared out of a deep conviction that the Word of God has something vital to say to people living in the twentieth century. Furthermore, the author believes that the Bible should be studied outside the seminary classroom and the church Sunday school. It is hoped, therefore, that they will encourage men in many walks of life to turn to the Scriptures in search of truth and light.

The Scripture quotations used are taken from the Revised Standard Version of the Bible. In this connection it should be noted that RSV stands for the Revised Standard Version and AV for the Authorized or King James Version.

The Theme of Amos

The dominant theme of the Book of Amos is justice. Justice is often associated with righteousness, a word to which it is closely related in meaning. They both have a legal or forensic background. Whenever two parties appeared before a judge to argue their case, a verdict was rendered in favor of one and against the other. Every trial ended in the victory of one party and the defeat of the other. To the loser the Hebrews applied the term commonly translated "wicked," and to the winner that which is normally rendered "righteous." In the early history of the Hebrews, these court terms did not imply a moral judgment; they simply designated the winner

6

and the loser.

In later usage, however, this was changed. The "righteous" was no longer simply the party who won the case, but rather the one who on ethical grounds *ought* to have won it. Thus "to justify" came to mean "to declare to be in the right," while "to condemn" meant "to declare to be in the wrong." If for any reason a judge "condemned" the righteous and "justified" the wicked, thus ignoring the true character of those who stood before him, he brought condemnation upon himself (Exod. 23:6-8; Lev. 19:15, 35; I Kings 8:31f.; Isa. 5:23). When justice was thus perverted in the law courts, this was "an abomination to the Lord" (Prov. 17:15), an act wholly incompatible with His nature and will as these had been made known to Israel.

The first charge Amos brings against the Israelites is that they "sell the righteous for silver, and the needy for a pair of shoes" (2:6; cf. 8:6). This meant that the rich man invariably secured a favorable verdict in the courts, though it cost him but a piece of silver or the trifling price of a pair of sandals. Amos was incensed when he saw this miscarriage of justice. So long as it continued he had no choice but to lift up his voice in portest.

> Hate evil, and love good, and establish justice in the gate; it may be that the Lord, the God of Hosts, will be gracious to the remnant of Joseph (5:15).

> I hate, I despise your feasts, and I take no delight in your solemn assemblies. Even though you offer me your burnt offerings and cereal offerings, I will not accept them, and the peace offerings of your fat beasts I will not look upon. Take away from me the noise of your songs; to the melody of your harps I will not listen. But let justice roll down like waters and righteousness like an everflowing stream (5:21-24).

One of the most misunderstood aspects of the prophetic preaching is this emphasis on social justice. There can be no doubt that in the time of Amos the situation demanded that he condemn Israel for her acts of injustice and oppression. Today, however, there are many who sincerely believe that such preaching falls outside the range of the minister's responsibility. To them it smacks of the "social gospel," which they regard as the antithesis of the true gospel.

That such an antithesis is false ought not to call for demonstration. Imagine Amos being told that he must not concern himself with social problems—with dishonesty in the courts and in the marketplaces, with the oppression of widows and orphans, with the immorality of organized religion! James D. Smart has noted in *The Old Testament in Dialogue with Modern Man* that:

> Too often those who advise the preacher to confine his attention to the souls of men and to keep his hands off such unspiritual matters as politics, economics, and the problems of society are not concerned for the spirituality of religion so much as for their own freedom to do as they please in social, economic, and political matters without hearing any restraining or rebuking word from the pulpit.

At the same time one must recognize the danger of a secularized social ethic. Some would adopt the ethic of Amos but reject his theology. There are those who admire the teachings of Jesus but will not accept His atonement. Against this kind of "social gospel" there is a legitimate protest. To follow this road is to fail to realize that the prophet's ethic was grounded in his theology. A purely secularized social ethic will always lack the dynamic that one encounters in the prophets. They became crusaders for justice precisely because their knowledge of God demanded that they do so.

Outline of the Book of Amos

The Book of Amos falls naturally into three divisions, after which there is an epilogue of hope.

(1) Chapters 1-2 serve as a preamble to the prophet's thesis: as other nations have courted disaster by breaches of the law of social righteousness, even so Israel faces imminent destruction. The messages in this first division have been fitted into a definite scheme or framework: "Thus saith the Lord: For three transgressions . . . yea for four, etc." (1:3, 6, 9, 11, 13; 2:1, 4, 6).

(2) Chapters 3-6 expand the prophet's charge against the people of Israel, who regard their prosperity as evidence of their righteousness and as proof of divine favor. The scheme into which these prophecies are fitted appears in 3:1; 4:1; and 5:1: "Hear this word, etc."

(3) Chapters 7:1—9:10 describe the visions which God gave to Amos foretelling pestilence, earthquake, famine, and locusts, which were stern reminders to the people that they should return to God before some worse calamity should overtake them. Another scheme is evident in 7:1, 4, 7, and 8:1: "Thus the Lord God showed me."

(4) The book concludes with an epilogue of hope (9:11-15) in which is painted a glorious picture of the Golden Age to come, when God will be reconciled to His people and Israel's fertile soil will yield bumper crops.

Contents

1

The Shepherd
Hears a Roar

Amos 1:1, 2

Amos' Background

The century in which Amos lived has been called the Golden Age of Hebrew prophecy, for it produced four great prophets, Amos and Hosea in Israel, and Isaiah and Micah in Judah.

The name Amos is derived from a verb meaning "to carry a load." It occurs in the Old Testament only in the Book of Amos. Amos the prophet should not be confused with Amoz, the father of Isaiah (Isa. 1:1).

Amos came from Tekoa, a village some ten miles south of Jerusalem. It was situated 2,500 feet above sea level and commanded an awesome view looking east toward the Dead Sea and the Wilderness of Judea. Tekoa is mentioned elsewhere in the Old Testament in II Samuel 14:2; 23:26; II Chronicles 11:6; Nehemiah 3:27; and Jeremiah 6:1. The word itself is derived from a root meaning "to pitch a tent," or "to blow a trumpet." The first meaning is the probable derivation of the name, for it suggests a place where nomadic shepherds pitched their tents. This accords with the occupation which Amos followed before he became a prophet.

Amos is described in 1:1 as being "among the shepherds of Tekoa." The word translated "shepherds" is not the usual Old Testament word for one who followed this occupation. It is a rare word describing those who tended a special variety of dwarfed-sized sheep highly prized for their wool, a variety still known among the Arabs. This word for shepherd is applied to Mesha king of Moab in II Kings 3:4, where it means "sheep breeder" or "sheep owner." This suggests that Amos may have been the owner of flocks of sheep and thus a man of some standing in his community. It is further stated in 7:14-15 that he was "a herdsman" and that the Lord took him "from following the flock." Taken together these references give a clear picture of one whose profession was the care of sheep.

Norman H. Snaith in *Amos, Hosea and Micah* has pointed out that shepherds played an important role throughout Biblical history. The patriarchs, Abraham, Isaac, and Jacob, were shepherds. Moses was leading the flocks of Jethro when God called him to lead his people out of Egypt. David was tending sheep when God appointed him shepherd over Israel. Shepherds were the first to greet the Christ child on the night of His birth. Jesus was proud to identify Himself with these men of the past and to refer to Himself as the Good Shepherd.

Amos is further described in 7:14 as "a pincher of sycamores." The sycamore of Palestine is a type of fig tree that flourishes in the lowlands. It is a large tree with widespread branches. The figs grow in clusters attached to the bark of the branches near the trunk of the tree. They are small in size and insipid in taste. The word "dresser" or "pincher" is defined by the Hebrew lexicon as "one who nips the unripe sykamore-fig (with nail or iron) in order to promote the ripening." Others maintain that there are insects inside the figs and that the figs must be punctured so that these may escape; otherwise the fruit will not ripen properly. This writer can vouch for the fact that the sycamore-figs are infested with insects. Once while visiting the excavations at Ashdod he stopped at a large sycamore tree and picked a handful of the ripe figs. It was only after tasting one of them that he discovered that someone had failed to puncture it, and that the insect was still inside!

The occupations of Amos were lonely and dangerous ones but there can be no doubt that they played an important role in shaping his life and thought. John Paterson in *The Goodly Fellowship of the Prophets* describes this influence in vivid language:

> Amos was rooted in the desert. . . . The wide open spaces in which he lived are reflected in the amplitude of his spiritual vision. . . . All his similes and metaphors reflect the bare gaunt background of the desert. His task, too, was his teacher. He must be quick to detect the rustle of the gliding snake and know the way of the lion and the bear. Every sound in the desert is significant, and the shepherd must know its meaning. . . . The desert was the school of Amos, and in that school his powers of observation were developed and his faculties sharpened in high degree.

The Call of Amos

Nothing is known regarding the call of Amos except the terse statement in 7:15: "The Lord took me from following the flock, and the Lord said to me, 'Go, prophesy to my people Israel.'" There is no indication here as to the nature of the message which the prophet was to preach. It is clear, however, that from the outset he considered himself to be under the absolute control of One mightier than he. He had no other choice but to obey. The same thought is expressed in 3:8: "The lion has roared; who will not fear? The Lord God has spoken; who can but prophesy?"

This sense of divine compulsion is characteristic of the servants of God throughout the Bible. Moses went forth to face Pharaoh because he had met God at the burning bush and his reluctance had been overcome. The Book of Jonah tells the story of a prophet who vainly imagined that he could escape the call of God by fleeing to Tarshish. Jeremiah felt the word of God like an irresistible fire shut up in his bones. Jesus lived and worked under the same sense of divine compulsion and the words "I must!" were constantly on his lips (Luke 2:49; 4:43; John 9:4).

Amos lived and worked in Judah until he received his call to be a prophet. He then journeyed northward to deliver his prophecies against the house of Israel. His call came at one of the decisive moments in sacred history. It was the hour of decision for the Northern Kingdom, the hour when she must choose between life and death. She must either come to God in repentance or else prepare to meet Him in judgment. When Israel finally cast her lot for destruction and death, she had no one to blame but herself. Though her people lacked the disposition to hear, they nevertheless knew that a prophet had been among them. They rejected him, but they were never able to forget him.

Amos' Ministry

The title-verse (1:1) places the ministry of Amos in the reign of Jeroboam II (786-746 B.C.). This information is in accord with the events narrated in 7:10ff. The Book of Amos reflects a situation in which there is prosperity and unbounded optimism. This fact suggests that Amos was active during the middle part of Jeroboam's reign, after the political and commercial expansion of his kingdom but prior to the threatening ascendancy of Assyria under Tiglath-Pileser III.

16

Amos 1:2 supplies the additional information that Amos' ministry came "two years before the earthquake." This is an obvious attempt to date the ministry of the prophet more specifically. Calamities, such as earthquakes, leave a deep impression in the minds of people, and it is common even today to hear someone refer to an event as having occurred either before or after such a calamity. It is significant that Zechariah 14:6 cites an earthquake that came during the days of Uzziah king of Judah, implying that it was of unusual severity. This may well be the same earthquake referred to in Amos 1:2. Concerning the earthquake that came during Uzziah's reign, Josephus states that it took place at the precise moment that Uzziah went into the temple to offer incense to God (II Chron. 26:18-21).

Amos 8:9 refers to another natural phenomenon, an eclipse of the sun. Scientific calculations make it simple to ascertain that a total eclipse of the sun actually occurred in Israel on June 15, 763 B.C. On the basis of this bit of information and the other evidence discussed above, scholars have usually dated the beginning of Amos' ministry somewhere near 760 B.C. Others would suggest a date around 745 or 744 B.C., but this seems entirely too late.

How long Amos continued to prophesy is not known. J. Morgenstern in *Amos Studies I* would limit it to "one brief half-hour, beginning shortly before dawn and concluding a few minutes after sunrise on New Year's Day" at the celebration of the New Year Festival at Bethel in 751 B.C. It is unlikely that Amos' ministry was so short. It is possible that it may have ended with his encounter with Amaziah at the Bethel shrine (cf. 7:10-17), but this does not mean that it also had its beginning on this occasion. Amaziah had reported to Jeroboam, "Amos has conspired against you in the midst of the house of Israel; the land is not able to bear all his words" (7:10b). This verse at least implies that the prophet had preached for a considerable length of time, long enough for his words to spread throughout the land of Israel. Perhaps he had preached not only at Bethel but also at Samaria, Gilgal, Dan, and other religious centers within the territory of Israel. A conservative estimate of the length of his ministry would be from three to six months, and perhaps even longer. If the date suggested above is correct, then Amos is the first of the canonical prophets.

Amos probably began his ministry at Bethel at a time when the tribes of Israel were assembled for one of their religious festivals. The prophets, as well as Jesus, liked to address themselves to the people on such occasions. It was then that the people were most receptive to religious truth.

The thesis of the prophet is clearly discernible as one studies these chapters. Amos believes that God's rule extends to all nations and that the standard by which the nations are judged is the standard of absolute justice. The nations have brought condemnation upon themselves by disregarding this standard. Israel is the most guilty of all and her punishment will be commensurate with her guilt.

Life in the Northern Kingdom 700 B.C.

Amos, who lived and worked as a shepherd in Judah in the eighth century B.C., was called to be a prophet to Israel, the Northern Kingdom. His work, therefore, must be understood against the background of the historical developments of this period. It was a decisive era for it witnessed the decline and fall of Israel.

The last half of the ninth century (850-800 B.C.) was a relatively quiet and uneventful period in Israel's history. The land was recovering from the blood purge of Jehu against Ahab, Jezebel, and the followers of Baal, which had been carried out in 842 B.C. While this purge had eliminated the immediate threat of Baalism, it had also left Israel weak and confused. The liquidation of the dynasty of Omri had deprived her of her most able leaders and administrators. It is a proven fact that reform movements seldom achieve their objectives, for as soon as the reformers are installed in office they, too, succumb to the temptations of power and corruption.

By having slain Jezebel, the daughter of the king of Tyre, and Ahaziah, the king of Judah, Jehu had alienated himself from both Tyre and Judah, formerly his country's staunchest allies. This so weakened Jehu's position that he was forced to pay tribute to Shalmanezer III of Assyria in 841 B.C. During the same period, Syria rose to new power under the able leadership of Hazael (842-806 B.C.), and began to threaten Israel's security.

When the eighth century dawned, Israel's fortunes took a turn for the better. This reversal of circumstances was caused by two factors: (1) able leaders, and (2) a changed world situation. The world situation changed when Syria was crushed by the Assyrian armies in 802 B.C. Fortunately, the Assyrians were unable to capitalize on their conquest of Syria or to pose a new threat to Israel.

Able leadership was provided when Jeroboam II (786-746 B.C.) came to the throne in Israel, to be followed shortly by Uzziah (783-742 B.C.) in Judah. This fortunate combination of circumstances prepared the way for an era of peace and unprecedented prosperity in Israel as well as in Judah. Jeroboam restored

Israel's borders from the entrance of Hamath to the Dead Sea (II Kings 14:25). This implies that the whole region of Transjordan was brought under his control. No king in Israel had ever reigned over so vast a territory. At the same time Uzziah was regaining control over Edom and reopening the port and industries of Ezion-geber (II Kings 14:22). Since Israel and Judah were at peace with each other, they could effectively control the major trade routes, exacting tolls from the caravans and enriching the treasuries of both countries. The opening of the port of Ezion-geber also made possible the revival of the lucrative Red Sea trade.

It seems to be axiomatic that when a nation prospers materially and begins to feel secure it falls into moral decay. Arnold Toynbee has shown this to be true throughout the six thousand years of recorded history. According to him, there have been twenty-one successive civilizations during the history of mankind. These have risen and fallen with monotonous regularity. Birth, growth, breakdown, disintegration—these are the steps that can be traced in the rise and fall of each civilization. There are many indications that Western Civilization has now reached the stage of breakdown, a stage which, if not arrested, will inevitably lead to total disintegration. It is a sobering thought to realize that we may soon take our place in the graveyard of dead civilizations. And, as Toynbee has demonstrated, breakdown is caused not by external enemies but by internal decay and corruption.

Such was the situation that Amos faced in Israel. The splendor of the reigns of Jeroboam and Uzziah was based on a concentration of wealth in the urban centers and not on the general welfare of all of society. Until now society had been predominantly agricultural. Its transformation into an urban society brought grave dangers—economic inequalities, class distinctions, indifference to human need and to social injustice, corruption in the courts, sexual immorality practiced in connection with and even in the name of religion. Israel had grown "prosperous, pious, and pitiless."

Israel had indeed grown prosperous. Her merchants were reaping rich profits (8:4-5). The privileged classes were able to build winter houses and summer houses and to furnish them with finely upholstered couches inlaid with ivory (3:12, 15; 6:4). They were able to provide the most expensive commodities such as high-grade veal and mutton for their feasts (6:4-6). These feasts featured private orchestras playing the latest versions of popular songs. Such wealth and the leisure to enjoy it had filled them with a false sense of security. A series of calamities described in Chapter 4—food shortages, droughts, locusts, and epidemics—had failed to dampen the spirit of optimism. Apparently, the people saw no connection between these occurrences and the moral character of the nation.

Israel had also grown pious. Prosperity had been accompanied by a religious revival. Pilgrims flocked to the sacred shrines at Bethel and Gilgal (4:4f.; 5:4f.). Some of the more zealous even made pilgrimages to the patriarchal shrine at Beer-sheba in southern Judah (5:5). The altars were piled high with sacrifices, and the temple treasuries overflowed with tithes and offerings. The worship was rich and beautiful, especially at the royal shrine at Bethel (7:13). The worshipers came not out of a sense of constraint but because they loved to do so (4:5).

There was also a note of expectancy in the air. Eschatological hopes ran high. Did not the favorable present presage an even more glorious future? "Strength for today and bright hope for tomorrow" must have been their theme song. There was an intense longing for the Day of the Lord, the consummation of the ages, when, according to popular expectation, God would be glorified and Israel vindicated (5:18-20). The people supposed that the coming of the Day of the Lord would bring honor to Israel and would usher in the Great Society. Amos, however, knew a mirage when he saw one, and he was not fooled by this outward show of religiosity. Religion can be an opiate of the people when it engenders false security and lulls them into thinking they have satisfied God's demands simply by being religious. Religion that places its sanction on the practices and customs of a corrupt society is worse than no religion at all: it is an affront to Almighty God.

Israel had become pitiless and unmerciful in her treatment of the poor. While the rich spared no expense in providing themselves with the choicest of wines, meats, and cosmetics, they were not grieved over "the ruin of Joseph" (6:6). This meant that they were insensitive to the suffering and distress of the vast majority of the people. In fact, they continued to enrich themselves at the expense of the poor whenever the opportunity arose. According to Amos justice had been denied the needy, the poor, and the afflicted (2:6ff.; 4:1; 5:11ff.; 8:4ff.). Unless God Himself intervened on their behalf, their situation would remain hopeless. The justice that should have prevailed in Israel had been turned into poison and bitter wormwood (5:7; 6:12). Against the growing luxury of the people, the injustices perpetrated upon the poor, and the flagrant immorality of religion, Amos became the protesting voice of an offended God. He saw no hope for Israel except in a return to God (see the refrain in 4:6, 8, 9, 10, 11; cf., 5:4, 6, 14) resulting in the establishment of justice and righteousness throughout the land. "But let justice roll down like waters and righteousness like an ever-flowing stream" (5:24).

These years have been described as Israel's Indian-summer, that deceptive period of warm, balmy weather that precedes the coming of winter. But when the day of reckoning came, it came swiftly. Jeroboam died a peaceful death in 746 B.C., after a reign of some forty years. His death, however, marked the beginning of the end. Within twenty-five years the Northern Kingdom ceased to exist. During this brief period the throne changed hands six times. This period of chaos has been described as a time "when one nobody after another seized the throne without even the pretense of legitimacy."

In addition to the anarchy and corruption within her own borders, Israel was threatened from without by the rising power of the Assyrians. In 745 B.C. Tiglath-Pileser III (745-727 B.C.) inaugurated a new period in history known as the period of the Assyrian Empire. This diabolically clever ruler led his army to sweeping victories in a war of total conquest. In 734 B.C., at the urgent request of Ahaz (II Kings 16:5-9), he attacked Syria and Israel. A year later Damascus, the capital of Syria, fell into his hands and was destroyed. Israel would have suffered a similar fate had she not surrendered. As the price for peace she had to pay the Assyrians a heavy annual tribute or ransom. The next two Assyrian kings, Shalmaneser V (727-722 B.C.) and Sargon II (722-705 B.C.), renewed the attack when Israel's king dared withhold this tribute. The end came in 721 B.C., when Samaria fell and, according to the annals of Sargon, 27,290 of her citizens were deported to Upper Mesopotamia and Media, from whence they never returned.

The Title-Verse (1:1)

This verse is similar to those found at the beginning

of other prophetical books (cf. Isa. 1:1; Jer. 1:1-3; Hos. 1:1; Mic. 1:1). These title-verses appear in the third person, indicating that they were not written by the prophets themselves. They were probably added to the finished collections of the prophets' messages by unknown scribes or editors who wished to furnish the reader with additional pertinent information about each prophet. The reference to the king of Judah in the opening verse of Amos suggests that this was written by someone living in the Southern Kingdom.

There is a mixture of metaphors in the clause, "the words . . . which he saw." Only a prophet could see a word! There was an intimate relation between vision and word in the prophets, between that which they saw and spoke. Whenever they spoke, it was because they had seen something and heard something.

In this verse Amos' ministry is dated "two years before the earthquake." There is an ominous note in this terse statement. Did the prophet perhaps prophesy concerning the earthquake before it struck? In 9:1 he speaks of God's smiting the pillars of the Bethel sanctuary so that the thresholds shake and the building crashes about the heads of the worshipers. If this prophecy is dated early in Amos' ministry, then the prophet is announcing the destruction of Bethel before it takes place. When it did take place—when the earthquake struck—then the people remembered the words of the prophet. Amos had indeed spoken the truth. The world in which he lived needed to be shaken, and he knew that it would be shaken.

This earthquake must have been unusually severe, since it is referred to again in Zechariah 14:5: " . . . and you shall flee as you fled from the earthquake in the days of Uzziah king of Judah." Josephus (Antiquities,

IX, 10, 4) states that it occurred at the time when Uzziah went into the temple to offer incense and was smitten with leprosy (II Chron. 26:16ff.).

Introduction to the Message of Amos (1:2)

This verse also belongs to the introduction of the Book of Amos. It summarizes the entire message of the prophet. God is coming in fierce judgment. His coming will bring dire consequences to all areas of life. These will extend even to the pasture-lands and to the mountain ranges.

"The Lord shall roar from Zion, and utter his voice from Jerusalem." Two interpretation of this statement have been given. Some have seen it in a reference to the roaring of the lion. The same verb occurs in 3:8, which reads: "The lion has roared; who will not fear? The Lord God has spoken; who can but prophesy?" To one accustomed to the ways of the desert, the roar of the lion meant that the animal was even then leaping upon its prey. In like manner the prophet sees God coming in judgment, from which there can be no turning back. In the light of this interpretation, Amos' message has been described as "the Gospel of the Lion's Roar."

Others see in this statement a reference not to the lion's roar but to the crashing of thunder. In Hebrew the "voice of God" is often the equivalent of thunder. This can be seen in the parallel statements of Psalm 18:13: "The Lord also thundered in the heavens, and the Most High uttered his voice" (cf. also Ps. 29:3-9; Job 37:4-5). The Old Testament frequently portrays God using the storm as an instrument of judgment. In the light of this interpretation, Amos might well be called "the Prophet of Thunder."

Whether one interprets this as the roar of the lion or

the crash of thunder, the meaning is the same. God is coming in judgment and the guilty will find no way of escape.

The references to Zion and Jerusalem indicate that the author of this verse shared the view that the place of God's habitation with His people was in Jerusalem (cf. Deut. 12:5-7). It is "from Jerusalem" that He will utter His voice. This is, of course, one of those partial truths of which the Old Testament furnishes many examples. God is not confined to one city or to one sanctuary. Many centuries after Amos lived, at a place not far from Bethel, the Prophet from Nazareth declared that God may be found wherever men worship Him in spirit and in truth (John 4:21ff.).

As a consequence of God's judgment, "The pastures of the shepherds mourn, and the top of Carmel withers." The pastures are the meadows where the sheep graze and where at night, according to Psalm 23:2, they lie down. It is significant that Amos the shepherd is concerned about green meadows and mountain slopes. The "top of Carmel" is a term applied to the entire range of mountains extending inland from Mount Carmel by the sea, the scene of Elijah's contest with the prophets of Baal, toward Beth-shan, some twelve miles to the southeast. No part of Palestine was more fertile or beautiful. Its luxuriant trees had become proverbial (Isa. 35:2; Song of Sol. 7:6). In time of drought it was the last area to be affected. Therefore, when the top of Carmel withers, how much more dreadful will be the effects on the rest of the land!

QUESTIONS

1. What kind of a man was Amos? Discuss his style and approach.

2. How is our contemporary American culture similar to that which existed in Israel at the time of Amos?

3. Amos began his ministry with scathing attacks on Israel's neighbors. Do we tend to magnify the sins of others and fail to see our own? What remedies would you suggest for this situation?

4. Amos confronted the people with God's moral law. They were guilty of idolatry and social injustices. Are these sins prevalent in America today? Can you see evidences of such sins in your own neighborhood? If so, do you have a responsibility to remedy these conditions? How would you meet this responsibility?

5. Through Amos, the Lord "roars" like a lion about to pounce upon its prey. Does the Lord still roar through His servants today? If so, how?

2

Disaster Ahead
for Israel's Enemies

Amos 1:3—2:3

This section consists of a series of six messages condemning the nations that surround Palestine for their inhuman treatment of their fellow men. This is a classic example of the prophetical outcry against man's inhumanity to man. The assumption that underlies these messages is that all nations are accountable to God for their social actions. Hitherto, the Old Testament had addressed itself solely to Israel. Amos was the first to summon all nations to stand before the judgment seat of God.

That nations are accountable to God for their actions has often been overlooked. Modern evangelical Christians have emphasized individual sin and guilt almost to the exclusion of any notion of corporate guilt. The prophets did not make this mistake. Isaiah saw himself as a man of unclean lips, dwelling in the midst of a people of unclean lips. He knew that as an individual he must bear the responsibility not only for his own sins but also for the sins of the society in which he lived. Jesus taught men to pray, "Forgive us *our* trespasses."

This lack of a sense of corporate responsibility is one of the most disturbing features of modern times. It has led some to adopt a double code of ethics, one code for the group and another for the individual. They believe that as members of a group (gang, club, fraternity, labor union, nation, etc.) they may permit themselves to do things which they would never do if acting alone. A good illustration of this can be seen in what happened in Germany during the Nazi era. When a man like Adolph Eichmann had supervised the slaughtering of six million Jews, he felt that he had incurred no personal guilt, since he was acting under orders from his superiors. When he was brought to trial, his defense was based on the plea that "where there is no responsibility, there is no guilt." Such a plea does not free one from responsibility for the sins of the society in which he lives.

Perhaps it would not be too strong a statement to say that most sin today is corporate, but most concern with it is individual, and therefore oftentimes quite ineffective. Dr. Henry Grady has said, "We face the possibility that while rejoicing in our salvation as individuals we may be destroyed in the mass. And always in a mass destruction it is the individual who suffers most."

1. The Judgment of Damascus (Syria) (1:3-5)

In this prophecy against Syria it is Damascus the capital city that is singled out for judgment. In the thinking of the prophets the capital of a country was a symbol of the whole national life. As went the capital, so went the rest of the nation. When a stream is polluted at its source, it is polluted throughout its entire course. The sin of Damascus had contaminated all of Syria.

Syria (oftentimes referred to in the Old Testament as Aram) is mentioned first because in the century preceding Amos she had posed the most serious threat to the security of Israel. The people of Israel must have rejoiced when they heard the prophet calling for their most hated enemy to stand up and be judged.

These prophecies of judgment against the nations are

set in a very rigid framework. The framework consists of three parts that can be readily distinguished. They are (1) the formal arraignment of the guilty nations before the judgment bar of God, (2) the specific indictment brought against each defendant, and (3) the pronouncement of judgment upon the accused.

"Thus says the Lord, 'For three transgressions of Damascus, and for four, I will not revoke the punishment.'" This is the formal arraignment of Damascus, and it is repeated in each of the following passages without any variation, except in the naming of the defendant (cf. 1:6, 9, 11, 13; 2:1).

The reference to "three transgressions, and four" is not to be interpreted literally. It does not mean "three or four" transgressions. Nor does it mean "three plus four." If either of these were the correct interpretation, it would indicate that Damascus was being charged with a relatively small number of transgressions. Actually, the figure of speech which the prophet is using suggests a large but indefinite number of transgressions (cf. Ps. 62:11; Prov. 6:16; 30:15, 18, 21, 29; Isa. 17:6; Hos. 6:2).

The word *transgressions* originally meant "rebellions" or "revolts." It is the characteristic word for sin in the prophetical books. It has to do not with the breaking of a set of laws but with rebellion against a personal God. Its use stresses the prophetical view of religion as a personal relationship between God and His people. "Hear, O heavens, and give ear, O earth; for the Lord has spoken: 'Sons have I reared and brought up, but they have rebelled against me'" (Isa. 1:2). It was the prophet's task "to declare unto Jacob his transgression and unto Israel his sin" (Mic. 3:8).

There is another feature of the formal arraignments

that calls for clarification. It has to do with the phrase rendered thus in the various translations: "I will not turn away the punishment thereof" (AV); "I will not reverse it" (AJ); "I will not revoke the punishment" (RSV). A reader of the Authorized Version (King James) will note that the words "the punishment" are printed in italics. Whenever this occurs it means that the italicized words were not in the original manuscripts but were supplied by the translators. A literal translation of the Hebrew in this instance would be: "I will not turn it back." The object "it" is undefined. Perhaps it does refer to the punishment which inevitably follows sin. Or it may refer to the Word of the Lord which has been set loose in the world and which will not return unto Him until it has accomplished His purpose against evildoers (cf. Isa. 55:11).

The specific indictment brought against the Syrians was that they had threshed Gilead with threshing sledges of iron. Gilead refers to the territory east of the Jordan which was occupied by Israelites. The sledges of iron were sledges into whose runners iron spikes had been driven. These were then weighted down with stones and dragged about over the threshing floor in order to separate the grain from the chaff. In this case the sledge teeth that had been designed to thresh wheat had been used to mangle the flesh of Israelite prisoners of war.

In the time of Amos there were no international agreements regulating the treatment of prisoners of war. Even today when such agreements do exist they are often violated. If wars cannot be eliminated, they could at least be made more tolerable if nations will adhere to international agreements.

The pronouncement of judgment upon the condemned nation comes in verses 4 and 5. Here, as in each of the messages that follow (cf. 1:7, 10, 12, 14; 2:2, 5), it is stated that God will send fire and that the fire will devour the "palaces" of the city. What were these palaces? Some would take them to be the palatial dwellings of the rich. Others interpret them to be strongholds (cf., RSV) or fortifications within the city. This term appears twenty-seven times in the Old Testament, and its most frequent use is in connection with the defense of walled cities. Furthermore, there seems to have been some relationship between these structures and the walls themselves (cf. II Chron. 36:19; Ps. 48:13; 122:7; Lam. 2:7; etc.). It appears that they were either fortified towers or fortresses, and that they formed an integral part of the defense system of the walled cities. The translation "strongholds" is to be preferred, therefore, instead of "palaces."

Hazael, king of Syria from 842 until 802 B.C. (II Kings 8:7-13), was succeeded by his son, Benhadad III. These two kings are mentioned as representatives of the royal house in Syria. The Valley of Aven and Beth-eden were place names within Syria, but their exact location is uncertain. The bar of Damascus refers to the heavy iron bar which secured the gate of the city against invaders. This bar will be broken. Amos is declaring that the defenses of the city, be they ever so strong, will not protect its inhabitants against the judgment of God.

They will be captured and taken into captivity to Kir. The location of Kir is uncertain, but it is significant that, according to Amos 9:7, this was the land from which the Syrians had originally migrated. Now they are to be uprooted from Damascus and returned as captives to the land of their origin.

32

2. The Judgment of Gaza (Philistia) (1:6-8)

The second of the prophecies of judgment is directed against Philistia, another traditional enemy of the Hebrews. Philistia lay to the southwest of Israel and encompassed within its territory the cities of Gaza, Ashdod, Ashkelon, Ekron, and Gath. Amos mentions all of these except Gath, and there is no known explanation why he should have omitted it. The most likely suggestion is that it had already been destroyed.

The Philistines belonged to the wave of Sea Peoples that swept into the Middle East from the Mediterranean prior to 1000 B.C. According to Amos 9:7, the original home of the Philistines was Caphtor, usually identified with Crete. Egyptian records tell how the Philistines attempted to invade Egypt but were beaten back and forced to settle along the northern frontier of that country. The Old Testament tells how they struggled with the Hebrews for possession of the land of Canaan during the days of Samson, Samuel, Saul, and David. It was because of the Philistines that the land of Canaan came to be called Palestine.

The accusation brought against the Philistines was that "they carried into exile a whole people to deliver them up to Edom." In other words, they had depopulated entire cities in order to sell their inhabitants into slavery to the Edomites. Such behavior went beyond the normal rules of warfare and was motivated solely by greed.

The punishment of Philistia is described in verses 7 and 8. God will send fire upon the wall, or, better, "within the enclosure" of Gaza. He will cut off the inhabitants from Ashdod. The word rendered inhabitants in 1:5 and 1:8 means literally "the one sitting,"

33

and probably refers to the one sitting on the throne, that is, the king. This would agree with the parallel expression, "and him that holds the scepter." "To hold the scepter" clearly means to reign as king. The Lord will punish the leaders of the Philistines, upon whom rests the major share of responsibility for the crimes committed. The reference to the destruction of the remnant of the Philistines means that no one will escape. The leaders and all the people are to be annihilated.

3. The Judgment of Tyre (Phoenicia) (1:9-10)

Amos now turns toward Phoenicia, which lay to the northwest of Israel. The seaport of Tyre was the chief city in Phoenicia, and in the mind of the prophet it symbolized the entire country. The population of Phoenicia was made up largely of the descendants of the Canaanites who had been driven out of Palestine during the Hebrew Conquest. They had become a highly civilized people and had developed a prosperous economy based on sea trade. They appear in the pages of the Old Testament as skilled artisans and as prosperous merchants.

The religion of the Phoenicians was Baalism, their cheif deities being Baal and Ashtarte. This religion had a pernicious effect upon the Israelites. This was due largely to the efforts of Jezebel, the daughter of the king of Phoenicia, who had married Ahab, king of Israel (I Kings 16:31). This enterprising woman sought to make Baalism the religion of Israel, and she might have succeeded had it not been for the opposition of Elijah and Elisha.

The charge made against Tyre is that she "delivered up a whole people to Edom, and did not remember the covenant of brotherhood." This is the same charge brought against the Philistines (1:6). Tyre and Edom were partners in a slave trade that left entire villages uninhabited.

Tyre's guilt was even greater than that of Philistia, for she had done this in violation of a "covenant of brotherhood." Assuming that the victims of these slave raids were Israelites, the most natural interpretation of this passage is that Tyre had done this in violation of a treaty between her and Israel. There are examples of such treaties as early as the days of Solomon (I Kings 5:12). To the sin of cruelty Tyre had added that of treachery.

There is nothing particularly noteworthy about the announcement of Tyre's punishment. God will send fire within her walls and it will devour her strongholds. The prophecy of Amos was fulfilled in 332 B.C., when Alexander the Great destroyed the city after a siege of seven months. It is said that six thousand of her inhabitants were slain, two thousand were crucified, and thirty thousand were sold into slavery.

4. The Judgment of Edom (1:11-12)

Amos now turns to curse Edom, which lay to the southeast of Israel. This is only one of a series of Old Testament passages condemning this ancient rival of Israel (Obad. 10-15; Ps. 137:7; Ezek. 25:12-14; Mal. 1:2-4). Through Esau, the Edomites traced their ancestry back to Abraham (Gen. 25:29-30). This made them blood-brothers to the Israelites, but, as has been observed, few rivalries are as bitter as those between brothers.

Edom is condemned for his unbridled anger. "He pursued his brother with the sword, and cast off all pity, and his anger tore perpetually, and he kept his wrath for ever." This is a difficult verse to translate but its meaning is clear enough. Edom's attitude toward his brother has been one of hatred and contempt. Doubtless this passage refers to an actual instance of Edom's unbrotherly behavior which made a deep impression on the people but whose circumstances are unfamiliar to modern readers. It is unlikely that there is any further reference to this incident in the Old Testament.

Edom's sentence is expressed in the identical pattern of the preceding prophecies. Fire will fall upon Teman and devour the fortresses of Bozrah. Teman was the name of a small district within Edom, and Bozrah was an important city. History has recorded that the Maccabees contributed to the fulfilment of Amos' prophecy by waging a victorious war of revenge against Edom around 150 B.C. (I Mac. 5:3, 65). The nation was completely exterminated during the later conflicts of the Zealots against Rome. The desolate ruins of Petra, the capital of Edom, have ever since stood as a silent witness that God's word never fails.

5. The Judgment of Ammon (1:13-15)

Ammon lay east of Israel on the other side of the Jordan River. It was separated from Moab on the south by the River Arnon. According to Genesis 19:30-38, the Ammonites were descendants of Lot, the nephew of Abraham. Despite this tradition of a common origin, these two nations did not live together peaceably. According to the Old Testament, there was intermittent warfare between them throughout most of their history.

It is for her cruelty during one of these armed conflicts that Ammon is condemned. She is charged with "ripping up," or disemboweling, the pregnant women of Gilead. This barbarous practice is mentioned elsewhere, in II Kings 8:12 and 15:16. Ammon committed this gruesome act in order that she might enlarge her border, or, in other words, for territorial gain. Nations must always answer to God for acts of cruelty committed in wartime against helpless civilians. This guilt is compounded when the war is one of conquest.

As Ammon has sowed, so shall she reap. This is the meaning of verses 14 and 15. Ammon had waged war against the innocent in order to acquire their territory. Now a day of battle is decreed against her, and the territory for which she fought will be taken from her. Rabbah, her chief city, will be destroyed by fire and all its strongholds demolished. The day of judgment will come upon Ammon like a tornado, and her king and princes will be swept away into exile.

6. The Judgment of Moab (2:1-3)

Moab's indictment states that she "burned to lime the bones of the king of Edom." The Israelites would never burn a corpse except when some crisis prevented their providing a proper burial. Furthermore, they considered it sacrilegious to deny burial to anyone, even an enemy. According to ancient Semitic belief, the dead who received no proper burial, or whose grave was disturbed, found no resting place in Sheol. Every disaster befell the man who was not buried in the grave of his fathers. When the prophet Jeremiah wished to pronounce a curse on Jehoiakim, he did so by declaring that "with the burial of an ass he shall be buried, dragged and cast forth beyond the gates of Jerusalem" (Jer. 22:19), and that "his dead body shall be cast out to the heat by day and the frost by night" (Jer. 36:30).

Many ancient graves bore inscriptions invoking a curse upon those who dared disturb the dead who rested within. One Eshmunazar of Sidon, for example, prayed that he who desecrated his tomb "might have no root beneath, or fruit above, or any beauty among the living under the sun." This shows the enormity of the crime which Moab had committed. The Targum, an Aramaic paraphrase of the Old Testament, adds a gruesome note to this account. It states that the lime into which the bones of the king of Edom had been burned was used as plaster upon the walls of a Moabite house.

Moab's punishment will come in the tumultuous invasion of her territory by an unnamed enemy. Moab will be slain "amid uproar, amid shouting and the sound of the trumpet." Her ruler will be cut off and her princes slain. All of this takes place, not because of some deed of violence practiced against Israel, but because of violence done to Edom, the enemy of Israel. This serves to illustrate the moral and ethical impartiality of the Hebrew prophet.

With this prophecy against Moab the foreign oracles come to an end. The crimes charged against the surrounding nations are crimes against common decency. They are violations of the minimum standards that God demands of all nations.

The practice of pronouncing doom on one's enemies was widespread in the Ancient Near East. Similar oracles existed among the Egyptians, the Hittites, and the Babylonians. Of special interest in this respect are the Egyptian Execration Texts. These are texts inscribed on broken fragments of pottery bowls. Since their discovery they have been kept in the Berlin Museum. When they were published in 1929, it was recognized that they contained curses, or "execrations." The Egyptian practice of execration seems to have involved the writing on bowls of the names of the enemies to be cursed, together with the curses. Then in a solemn ceremony the bowls were smashed (cf. Jer. 19:10, where the prophet is told to break a potter's earthen vessel in the sight of the men of Jerusalem), and with the smashing of the bowls the curses were believed to become effective.

It has been pointed out that these prophecies of Amos are parallel in style to the Egyptian Execration Texts. These latter pronounce their execrations or curses first upon foreign nations, following the four corners of the earth, and then upon the enemies of the pharaoh living within Egypt itself. In like manner, Amos begins in the northeast with Damascus, then swings to Philistia in the southwest, then returns to Phoenicia in the northwest, and comes finally to the southeast to curse the Edomites and their neighbors, the Ammonites and the Moabites.

In pronouncing doom on Israel's enemies, Amos was following a well-known cultic pattern, but when he included Israel among the doomed he broke the pattern. And because he broke the pattern Israel came to regard him as a dangerous enemy.

QUESTIONS

1. Why did the Lord concern Himself with heathen nations? Does this mean anything to us today?
2. Name and discuss the specific crimes of which the six nations mentioned were guilty. How do these compare with the atrocities which we read about in Indo-china and other modern struggles?
3. Granted that Christians have a responsibility to enter into the struggles of others to gain human rights, how far does this responsibility extend? Must Christians necessarily give leadership to such movements? Is financial support enough?

4. Are there inherent dangers in a socially-related church ministry?

5. How can socially minded Christians maintain rapport with fellow church members whose main concern is personal piety? How can a better understanding be developed between these two points of view?

3
Judah and
Israel Indicted

Amos 2:4-16

1. The Judgment of Judah (2:4-5)

The people can hardly believe their ears when Amos prophesies against his own nation. Of even greater significance is the charge brought against Judah, for it is precisely the charge she would have made against Israel: "They have rejected the law of the Lord and have not kept his statutes."

The people of Judah would have vehemently denied this charge. Did they not have the Mosaic law, the Aaronic priesthood, the Solomonic temple, and the Davidic kingship? How, then, could anyone accuse them of rejecting the law of the Lord? It is certain that if Amos had prophesied in Judah he would have been rejected even as he was in Israel.

Amos further accuses Judah of idolatry. This is the meaning of the statement that "their lies have caused them to err." The word translated lies often refers to false gods. It occurs in Psalm 40:4, for example, where it is translated: "Blessed is the man who makes the Lord his trust, who does not turn to the proud, to those who go astray after false gods!" (RSV). According to Amos, one who goes after a false god is led astray. Idolatry is self-deception. Furthermore, idolatry is contagious: the people of Judah are following the same gods after which their fathers walked.

Judah's sentence is stated in the stereotyped form common to these prophecies. Fire will fall upon Judah and devour the strongholds of Jerusalem.

The Judgment of Israel (2:6-16)

Amos had shrewdly led up to the climax of his sermon. A thrill of excitement swept over his listeners as one by one he condemned their hereditary enemies. But they were unprepared for the shock that came when he asked them to condemn themselves.

E. Stanley Jones relates this interesting occurrence:

> An Indian student came to a friend of mine and told him of a new society they had formed, "The Society for the Confession of Sins." My friend was interested in such a novel society and suggested that it must be very difficult to confess their sins to each other in this way. "Oh, no," replied the youth, "it is not difficult, for we don't confess our own sins, but other people's sins."

In this prophecy against Israel there is a good example of what has been called a covenant lawsuit. This is a device designed to restore a breach of covenant and is to be distinguished from a covenant renewal ceremony. Examples of such lawsuits can be seen in almost all of the pre-exilic prophets (cf. Isa. 1:2ff.; 3:13ff.; 5:1-7; Jer. 2:1ff.; Hos. 2:2ff.; 4:1ff.; Amos 3:1-2, 9-15; 4:1ff.; Mic. 6:1ff.).

These covenant lawsuits included some or all of the following elements: (a) A call to the witness to give an ear; (b) An introductory statement by the Divine Judge or His prophet; (c) A recital of the gracious and marvelous acts of God; (d) A recital of calamities and judgments in the recent past which should have recalled the people to God; (e) The specific indictment; (f) The sentence.

The role of the prophets in these lawsuits is highly significant. They literally believe that they are officers of the heavenly court sent to announce that God's covenant has been breached and that radical judgment is forthcoming. After announcing the divine sentence, which is usually very short, the prophets may expound on this, categorizing the sins of the people. Or they may undertake to substantiate their own call and authority to be prophets. At other times they engage in lamentation and intercession for the people. This last point is important since in the Old Testament the function of intercessor belongs not to the priests but to the prophets.

The arraignment of Israel is couched in the same terms as in the preceding passages and is followed immediately by the indictment. In this case, however, the indictment is much longer than usual, extending from verse 6 through verse 8.

The first charge Amos brings against the Israelites is that they sell the righteous for silver and the needy for a pair of shoes. This may mean either that the creditors were selling their debtors into slavery in order to collect the most trivial debts, or that the rich invariably gained a favorable verdict in the courts, though it cost them but a piece of silver or the price of a pair of sandals. What Amos condemns here is the survival of the slickest!

Verse 7 is extremely difficult to translate or interpret. The AV reads:

> That pant after the dust of the earth on the head of the poor, and turn aside the way of the meek: and a man and his father will go in unto the same maid, to profane my holy name.

The RSV is quite different, especially in the first part of the verse:

> They that trample the head of the poor into the dust of

the ground, and turn aside the way of the afflicted; a man and his father go in to the same maiden, so that my holy name is profaned.

The first verb is used in the Old Testament with the meaning "to pant" (Ps. 119:113; Isa. 42:14; Jer. 14:2), "to sniff" (Jer. 2:24), or "to long for" (Job 7:2; 36:20). The first meaning was adopted by the translators of AV. If this translation is accepted, then the expression may be interpreted to mean that they were so land hungry that they begrudged the poor the dust that settled on their head, perhaps sprinkled there as a sign of mourning. This interpretation seems to read too much into the words of the prophet.

The translation of RSV reflects a different interpretation. The verb can also mean "to trample, to crush" (cf. Gen. 3:15; Ps. 56:2; 57:3; Ezek. 36:3; Amos 8:4). The RSV in Amos 8:4 reads: "Hear this, you who trample upon the needy. . . ." In the light of this verse, perhaps Amos 2:7 would best be translated: "They that trample the head of the poor into the dust of the earth." This translation has the support of the Septuagint and the Vulgate. One might compare the words of Amos with those of his contemporary, Isaiah: "What do you mean by crushing my people, by grinding the face of the poor? says the Lord God of hosts" (Isa. 3:15).

"To turn aside the way of the afflicted" means to deny justice to the afflicted. The afflicted are not the sick and diseased but rather the oppressed. Amos 5:12 repeats this accusation against the judges of Israel; they "turn aside the needy in the gate." Justice was usually dispensed by the elders who would be seated "in the gate" at the entrance to the city. However, Amos saw that the place of justice had become the place of oppression.

The last half of verse 7 refers to religious prostitution, a degrading practice borrowed from the Canaanites. To understand the existence of such a practice one needs to remember that the religion of the Canaanites was a nature religion and that the Canaanite pantheon included both gods and goddesses. The chief function of every nature-god, and of Baal in particular, was to maintain the processes of nature in harmonious balance and to promote fertility in the fields, among the flocks, and in the females of each tribe. The Canaanites did not know the meaning of such terms as over-production, food surplus, and population explosion!

There were many ways in which the people prevailed upon Baal to fulfil his function. One way was to declare a certain number of women "holy," set apart to serve as prostitutes at the Baal shrines. To do this was to place the fertility of women, and symbolically, that of the land and herds under the maintenance and protection of Baal.

The practice of religious prostitution, whether by men or women, was forbidden in Israel (Deut. 23:17-18). It was considered an abomination, that which was grotesquely out of harmony with the revealed character and will of Israel's God. The prophets, in particular, looked with horror upon this gross sexual aspect of Canaanite religion (cf. Jer. 2:20-24; Hos. 4:12-14).

There is a sex-cult in America today that in many respects would put Baalism to shame. In his book, *The American Sex Revolution,* Harvard sociologist Pitirim A. Sorokin states that our civilization has become so preoccupied with sex that it now "oozes from all the pores of American life." He warns us that history has demonstrated that sexual license is a very effective tool for destroying a civilization, whereas a strong civilization cannot be built without sexual restraint. Sorokin sees a close parallel between the sex habits of ancient Egypt, Greece, and Rome during their decadent years and the present sex revolution in America. The Canaanites had a purpose—not altogether unworthy—in what they did, but the modern sex-cult has no philosophy except the gratification of animal instincts.

In the translation of 2:7 in AV, the word "same" is printed in italics, which means that it is not found in the Hebrew manuscripts. The definite article stands with the word "maiden," indicating that "the maiden" represents the whole class of temple prostitutes. The verb "to go" is in the imperfect state in the Hebrew, thus describing that which is done repeatedly. The mention of both father and son means that the practice was universal. Both young and old went regularly to the temple prostitutes.

It should be emphasized that this was being done not at some Baal shrine but at Israelite temples dedicated to the worship of God—at Bethel, at Dan, and at Gilgal. The Israelites had borrowed this vile practice from the Canaanites and had incorporated it into their worship of God. This meant that they had reduced Him to the level of Baal, that they regarded Him as little more than a nature-god. Thus they had profaned His holy name. In Scripture the name of God stands for God Himself. It is the equivalent of the sum of His attributes as these have been revealed to His chosen people (cf., Exod. 20:7; Ps. 111:9; Isa. 57:15; Matt. 6:9). Jesus taught His disciples to pray, "Hallowed be thy name."

The licentious behavior of the Israelites was closely related to their oppression of the poor. Verse 8 makes this clear: "They lay themselves down beside every altar upon garments taken in pledge; and in the house of their

God they drink the wine of those who have been fined." The "garments taken in pledge" were those which the rich had taken from the poor as collateral for loans. The law specified that such pledges were to be returned to their owners at sundown so that these might have cover during the night (Exod. 22:26-27). In open violation of this stipulation, the men of Israel kept the garments and used them for their own shameful purposes. Furthermore, they drank wine during their nocturnal orgies, and it, too, had been obtained by the oppression of the poor, through fines imposed on them by these men of distinction. The drunkenness and licentiousness of the Israelites bring to mind the behavior of Noah (Gen. 9:20ff.). It is possible that Noah was a symbol of the Israelites who had fallen victim to the licentious Baal worship of Canaan. This may explain why, on the occasion of Noah's drunkenness, a curse was placed upon Canaan.

Having stated the charge against Israel, the prophet now recounts the gracious and marvelous acts of God on her behalf (verses 9-12). What had God done for Israel? First, He had brought her out of Egypt (verse 10a). The prophets looked to the exodus from Egypt as to no other event in the past as the revelation of the gracious concern of God for His people (cf. Hos. 11:1, Mic. 6:3-4). This was the prime source of Israel's obligation to God (cf. Exod. 20:1-2).

God had also preserved Israel forty years in the wilderness (v. 10b). In Deuteronomy 1:19 the wilderness is referred to as "that great and terrible wilderness." Anyone who has stood on the hills above the Dead Sea and gazed southward across this heat-seared wasteland can begin to understand these words. The prophets often pictured the period of wilderness wanderings as Israel's honeymoon period (cf. Jer. 2:2, 6; Hos. 9:10; 13:5).

Isaiah 63:14 describes God's purpose in the gracious leading of His people: "Like cattle that go down into the valley, the Spirit of the Lord gave them rest. So thou didst lead thy people, *to make for thyself a glorious name.*"

The third of the mighty acts of God is described in verse 9, which, incidentally, seems to be out of its chronological order. It probably should come after verse 10, since the exodus from Egypt (verse 10) preceded the conquest of Canaan (verse 9). The conquest of Canaan is accomplished not the Israelites but by their God. It was He who destroyed the Amorites, those ancient inhabitants of Palestine, renowned for their height and for their prowess in warfare (Num. 13:32-33; Deut. 1:28). According to Numbers 13:29, the inhabitants of the south were called Amalekites, those who dwelt in the Jordan Valley and along the coast were called Canaanites, while those who dwelt in the hills were known as Hittites, Jebusites, and Amorites.

God not only delivered His people from bondage, led them through the wilderness, and brought them into the promised land, but He also raised up religious leaders for their guidance and instruction. Two groups of leaders are mentioned in verse 11: the prophets and the Nazirites. The prophets were to be the spokesmen of God, interpreting His will to Israel. This was a special mark of divine favor, because it was the prophetic ministry more than anything else that distinguished Israel from her neighbors. The Nazirites (cf. Num. 6:1-21), like the Rechabites (cf. Jer. 35:1-19), dramatized their protest against Canaanite culture and religion by refusing to cut their hair or to use any kind of intoxicating beverage. They distrusted Canaanite civilization in all of its aspects and pleaded for a return to the simple nomadic life, the life Israel had known in the desert before she entered Canaan. In many ways they were similar to the Amish groups still found in certain parts of the United States.

By raising up prophets and Nazirites from among the sons of Israel, God sought to keep before His people the demands of the covenant He had made with them at Sinai. Israel would always be reminded of these demands as the prophets proclaimed His word and as the Nazirites held up the ideal of a simple and devout life.

But Israel would not have it so! Unwilling to follow their God-given leaders, they made the Nazirites drink wine and commanded the prophets to be silent. They made the Nazirites drink wine! A drunken society could not tolerate such a group as this in their midst. So, whether by force or by persuasion, they made the Nazirites drink wine. Instead of following the example of the Nazirites, the Israelites succeeded in bringing the Nazirites down to the Israelites' level. This is still the way the world deals with those who stand for an ideal or a principle. It seeks to destroy its idealists by persuading them to compromise their principles; they then become indistinguishable from the mass of humanity. Thus society is no longer disturbed by those who would speak to its conscience.

Israel also commanded the prophets to be silent. They were saying in effect that they could get along without any word from the Lord. This was the last stage of their alienation from God. Amos spoke here out of bitter experience, for he had been told that he must never again prophesy at Bethel (7:12-13). But Israel was to learn that when men reject the word of God, the time comes when they can no longer hear it. This was to be their punishment, as it is described in 8:11-12:

"Behold, the days are coming," says the Lord God,

49

"when I will send a famine on the land; not a famine of bread, nor a thirst for water, but of hearing the words of the Lord. They shall wander from sea to sea, and from north to east; they shall run to and fro, to seek the word of the Lord, but they shall not find it."

Israel was guilty of corrupting her idealists and suppressing those who would speak the truth to her. What an indictment against a nation for whom God had done so much! For such a guilty nation there was a stern word of judgment. The prophet pronounces sentence upon her in verses 13-16.

The Hebrew of verse 13 is uncertain. According to AV the verse should read: "Behold, I am pressed under you, as a cart is pressed that is full of sheaves." According to this translation, the verse teaches that God feels the sin and injustice of Israel as a weight which He must carry, comparable to the weight carried by a fully-loaded wagon at harvest time. A similar thought is expressed in Isaiah 43:24b: "But you have burdened me with your sins, you have wearied me with your iniquities" (cf. Isa. 1:14).

Another possible translation is that adopted by RSV: "Behold, I will press you down in your place, as a cart full of sheaves presses down." In the light of this translation the verse refers to the time of threshing, when a heavily loaded wagon was pulled across the sheaves lying on the threshing floor (cf. Isa. 28:27-28). God will crush the nation as the wagon would crush the grain under its wheels. The allusion is probably to an invading army in whose wake the Israelites would suffer defeat.

The next three verses (14-16) describe an invasion, with the defending army in full and disorderly retreat. While Amos does not mention the pursuing force, he doubtless had the Assyrians in mind. Before the fury of the enemy all units of Israel's army, including the infantry (14), the artillery (15a), and the cavalry (15b), will turn in headlong flight. Even the courageous men will discard everything that might hinder their flight—weapons, armor, or even superfluous clothes—and will flee away naked in that day (16).

Thus saith the Lord!

QUESTIONS

1. How does the condemnation of Judah differ from the charges made against the heathen nations?
2. Discuss specific ways that Christians can combat the growing tendency toward apostasy. Do you feel that the use of a less structured or unstructured worship service is a helpful or harmful practice?
3. Which sins are listed in Israel's indictment?
4. What is the Biblical basis for human rights? Do human rights change?
5. Do you feel that some businessmen take advantage of the poor today? If so, how can such abuses be corrected?
6. Do some Christians show ingratitude for their salvation? How?
7. Israel told the prophets not to prophesy. Do church members today restrict their pastors in proclaiming the Word? If so, in what ways?
8. Why is it important to pass on a religious, cultural, and moral heritage to succeeding generations?

4
Plain Words
from the Prophet

Amos 3

In Chapters 3-6 Amos expands his charges against the people of Israel. While they look upon their prosperity as evidence of their righteousness and as proof of divine favor, he reminds them that God's goodness is due to no merit on their part and only serves to increase their responsibility. Three times in these chapters one encounters the solemn exhortation "Hear this word!" (3:1; 4:1; 5:1). For convenience of handling, the materials in Chapters 3—6 will be divided into two parts, 3:1—4:13 and 5:1—6:14.

Israel's Election and Its Corollaries (3:1-2)

Though these verses are very brief, they probably contain the essence of one of the sermons of Amos.

> Hear this word that the Lord has spoken against you, O people of Israel, against the whole family which I brought up out of the land of Egypt: "You only have I known of all the familieis of the earth; therefore I will punish you for all your iniquities."

The prophet again reminds Israel of her rescue from slavery in Egypt and of her election to be the people of God. The Hebrew verb "to know" can be used for any type of knowledge, but it usually refers to knowledge based on personal acquaintance and intimate relationship. It is used, for example, to describe the most intimate of personal relationships, the husband's sexual knowledge of his wife (Gen. 4:1). Stemming from this emphasis upon personal knowledge, the verb may sometimes mean "to choose" (cf. Gen. 18:19, Jer. 1:4). Amos doubtless had in mind God's election of Israel when he said, "You only have I known."

The whole subject of election has created considerable discussion. To some, God's election of Israel is the scandal of the Old Testament. J. A. Sanders in *The Old Testament in the Cross* has described this anomaly in these words:

> God in choosing a people selects Israel, a bunch—not even a proper nation, mind you!—a bunch of slaves building the store cities of the Egyptian Pharaoh toward the end of the fourteenth century B.C. Frankly the selection is a bit of a disappointment. Forgive the analogy, but suppose you were God and you were choosing a people for the job. Why, of course, you would choose Egypt. So would I. You wouldn't need a team of efficiency experts to help you make the decision. Egypt had the biggest army, the greatest wealth, and the most influence in the world at the time. They could have done the job in no time flat. Pharaoh could have issued a royal decree to the effect in all his provinces, and to unconquered lands he could have dispatched his armies with a zeal inspired of a holy mission. . . . Pharaoh was in a position to cram the message down the throat of every nation he could reach. . . . One's imagination fairly soars in thinking of the possibilities. . . . [But] God chose a people who were not a people, just a motley crew of slaves, to carry his message, to bless the world."

When one presses for an explanation for God's choice of Israel, he can find none more satisfactory than that given by the reformation theologians: "God loved Israel because God loved Israel." This means that the ground of Israel's choice was not in Israel but in God Himself. "I will be gracious to whom I will be gracious, and will show mercy on whom I will show mercy" (Exod. 33:19). God's ways are not our ways, and this is never more apparent than in His choice of those who will perform His services and proclaim His word. This was true not only under the old covenant but also under the new.

> For consider your call, brethren; not many of you were wise according to worldly standards, not many were powerful, not many were of noble birth; but God chose what is foolish in the world to shame the wise, God chose what is weak in the world to shame the strong, God chose what is low and despised in the world, even things that are not, to bring to nothing things that are, so that no human being might boast in the presence of God (I Cor. 3:26-29).

When one considers how proud many of us are of our own achievements, he wonders if we have not lost sight of the Biblical doctrine of election. When we attribute our success to our efficient agencies and institutions, to our stewardship programs, and to our well-trained leaders, we have forgotten that no human being should boast in the presence of God. When by our actions and our words we imply that we have reached the point where we can take over the job and relieve God of His responsibility, then we are dangerously near the point where God can no longer afford to use us at all. God has always been pleased to use the weak, but only so long as they acknowledged their weakness—never when they boasted of their self-sufficiency.

Why did God choose one nation from among all others? What is the purpose of election as it is set forth in the Old Testament? We have already seen that it was not because of Israel's inherent goodness. Neither was it because God loved other nations any less than He loved Israel; it was, rather, His purpose to choose one nation that through it all nations might be blessed and come to share in His salvation (cf. Gen. 12:1-3). Israel was chosen that she might be a kingdom of priests and a holy nation (Exod. 19:6). God had a message He wished to communicate to all mankind. Since the best way to send a message is to wrap it up in a person, God chose Israel to be His witness. When she forgot her mission and became involved in lesser tasks, God sent His prophets to announce that she had broken her covenant and forfeited her birthright.

When Amos declared that God had chosen Israel alone, the people readily accepted his interpretation of their history. They did not, however, agree with his definition of the corollaries of election. They would have said, "We are God's chosen people, therefore no harm can come to us. God is honor-bound to protect us, regardless of our character or conduct." The prophet said, "God has highly honored you and has chosen you above all nations. You have been willing to receive His blessings but you have ignored your responsibilities. Therefore, God will punish you in proportion to the way in which you have been blessed."

Because God had honored Israel in a unique way, the standard of judgment He applied to her was more exacting than that applied to other nations. Amos was enunciating a principle that was given classic expression by our Lord:

> And that servant who knew his master's will, but did not make ready or act according to his will, shall receive a severe beating. . . . Every one to whom much is given, of him will much be required; and of him to whom men commit much they will demand the more (Luke 12:47, 48b).

Election to privilege is always election to duty and to responsibility.

There is in this verse another truth of equal importance which may easily be overlooked. "You only have I known. . . ; *therefore* I will punish you. . . ." The judgment that is threatening Israel may be looked upon as further evidence of God's love and concern for her. God chastens Israel because He loves her, and because His love is stronger than her rebellion. When the end purpose of God's judgment is redemption, then judgment itself is but another manifestation of His love. Long ago a wise man wrote: "My son, do not despise the Lord's discipline or be weary of his reproof, for the Lord reproves him whom he loves, as a father the son in whom he delights" (Prov. 3:11-12).

The Lion Has Roared (3:3-8)

The most widely held view, and the one adopted here, is that in this passage Amos is seeking to establish his authority as a prophet. Perhaps he had been forced to do so by someone who challenged his right to speak in the name of the Lord. By means of a series of illustrations drawn from his experiences as a shepherd he seeks to establish the principle that every effect presupposes a cause, that is, that in God's universe everything has meaning.

"Do two walk together, unless they have made an appointment?" (v. 3). The Septuagint reads, "Will two walk together unless they know one another?" The Hebrew verb employed here means "to meet at an appointed place." If two men are seen crossing the trackless desert, it is certain that they have met by appointment. When men hear the roar of a lion, they know that he is leaping upon his prey. If he is growling, they know he has taken food to his den. If a bird swoops down from the heavens, they know that something has attracted its attention. If a trap springs up from the ground, they know that something has triggered it. In the world of nature everything has meaning.

Having established the principle that a known effect presupposes a knowable cause, the prophet now proceeds to show that certain causes always have predictable effects. The illustrations of this thesis are given in verses 6-8. They are drawn from the realm of history rather than from that of nature. They have a more ominous ring than the earlier illustrations and are also more pertinent to Israel.

When the trumpet sounds in the city (or, in modern terms, "when the air-raid warning sounds"), the people are frightened. The trumpet, or ram's horn, was blown to signal the approach of an enemy and to summon the men to arms. When calamity or misfortune (a better translation than "evil") overtakes a city, it is because God has done it. Amos shared the common view that God was the direct cause of all disasters, including those in the realm of nature.

Before God brings calamity against Israel, however, He always announces His purpose to His servants the prophets (v. 7). This verse is one of the most important in the Book of Amos for understanding the prophetic consciousness. It boldly claims that God reveals His secret purposes to the prophets. How God does this is not indicated. Nor should this be interpreted to mean that in the course of the world's history every great event has already been foretold in prophecy. Whatever may be the view one takes of this verse, the fact remains that from the time of Moses onward every great crisis in Israel's history was accompanied by the appearance of a prophet who sought to interpret the crisis in the light of his understanding of God's will and purpose. It was this that led Wellhausen to refer to the prophets as "God's storm-birds." The prophet's very presence among the people was a warning that God was coming in judgment and that they should prepare to meet Him.

According to verse 8, the prophet to whom God reveals His secret has an overwhelming sense of divine compulsion. "The lion has roared; who will not fear? The Lord God has spoken; who can but prophesy?" This sense of divine call is the hallmark of the Hebrew prophet. He found in his bones a fire burning, an inner constraint that he was unable to control (cf. Jer. 20:9ff.). In the Hebrew of verse 8, the lines are short and concise, creating the impression that Amos responded to the call of God with an emotion akin to fear and dread. Perhaps, like Moses and Jeremiah, he shrank back from such an unpleasant task only to discover that he was unable to say no to God.

The Israelites knew the meaning of the lion's roar, the downward flight of the bird, and the springing of a trap. They knew how to react to the trumpet's blast and to the lion's roar, but they failed to apprehend the significance of the appearance in their midst of a prophet of God. Amos made it clear that his coming was neither accidental nor trivial. A moment of great import had arrived. Within the lifetime of most of his listeners Israel would cease to exist. As in every great crisis, God had revealed His intentions to His prophet. The message that Amos proclaimed, therefore, was not his own. Necessity was laid upon him to proclaim the word of God and upon the people to give heed to it.

The Sins of Samaria (3:9—4:3)

With the exception of the oracle in 3:13-15, this

section deals with conditions as they existed in Samaria, the capital of the Northern Kingdom. In a series of messages that are short and perhaps fragmentary, the prophet attacks the corruption and injustice that existed at the very heart of Israel.

1. A Brief Lawsuit (3:9-10)

The covenant lawsuit theme is evident in this brief message. God summons witnesses to hear Him plead His case against Samaria, a city that has become notorious for its violence and oppression. The witnesses are the Philistines and the Egyptians, both ancient enemies of Israel. In spite of their pagan background, they will be shocked by what they see in Samaria. The meaning of verses 9b and 10b is that Israel's prosperity depends upon robbery and oppression. Their palaces are filled with goods that have either been stolen or seized by violence. Dr. John R. Sampey used to say that Amos snorted every time he saw a palace. Such a sight as this was enough to make a man snort!

The charge made against the nation in 10a is also a devastating one. "They do not know how to do right," says the Lord. This is a description of a nation sick unto death. The last state of depravity has been reached when conscience ceases to do its work and the sinner can no longer distinguish between right and wrong. H. Wheeler Robinson has described this as "the atrophy of the will." The sequel to disobedience is the growing inability to obey. When people will not do right, the time comes when they cannot do right.

2. The Approach of the Adversary (3:11-12)

These two verses provide a picture of total disaster.

An unidentified adversary will come upon Samaria from all sides. Her strongholds, which have served as store-houses for her ill-gotten gain, will be plundered and laid waste. The ruin produced will be complete—as complete as the destruction of a lamb caught by a lion, from whose mouth the shepherd rescues only two shank bones and a piece of an ear, which he would show to the owner of the flock as proof that the animal had indeed been slain and not sold (cf. Gen. 31:39; Exod. 22:13). This is Amos' doctrine of the remnant! It is a mutilated remnant, hardly worthy of the name.

The Hebrew of verse 12b is obscure. One suggested translation is: "that dwell in Samaria in the corner of a bed, and in Damascus on a couch" (so Septuagint and AV). This would mean that the inhabitants of Damascus were being condemned along with those of Samaria. Others would connect the word "Damascus" with a fine fabric originating in Damascus, sometimes referred to as damask. Thus ASV translates: "that sit in Samaria in the corner of a couch and on the silken cushions of a bed." The translators of RSV simply gave up and inserted the ambiguous word "part" in the place of "Damascus." However one translates this obscure word, it is evident that the prophecy is addressed to the luxury-loving nobles of Samaria who hide in their beds and couches when the invader comes.

3. The Judgment of Bethel (3:13-15)

This prophecy describes the fate of Bethel, one of the sanctuaries of Israel, situated some ten miles north of Jerusalem. It was here that Amos had his memorable encounter with Amaziah the priest (7:10ff.). Bethel was the royal shrine, analogous to Westminster Abbey in

Britain. It was hallowed by ancient traditions associated with the name of Jacob (cf. Gen. 28:18-22; 35:9-15). Bethel meant "house of God," and the people doubtless thought of it as just that.

Amos prophesied that Bethel's altar would be desecrated and its horns chopped off and cast to the ground. Because Bethel was the dwelling place of God, the prophet's words were blasphemous; because it was the king's sanctuary, they were seditious The horns of the altar were stone projections extending out from its four corners. According to ancient custom, anyone who in time of trouble fled to the altar and laid hold of the horns was granted asylum (cf. I Kings 1:50). In a similar manner the Israelites were accustomed to refer to God as the horn of their salvation (Ps. 18:2). When the prophet announced the cutting off of the horns of the altar, he was saying that there would be no place of refuge for Israel on the day of retribution.

The noblemen of Bethel had built warm houses for the winter season and summer houses for the hot dry season (v. 15). This may refer either to separate buildings (cf. Jer. 36:22), or to one building on two levels, the ground level for winter living, and the upper level for summer use (cf. Judg. 3:20). In any event, such buildings were regarded by the prophet as needlessly extravagant.

The men of Bethel had also decorated their houses with inlaid ivory. This is the meaning of the reference to "houses of ivory." In excavations carried out at Samaria between 1931 and 1935, the British archaeologist J. W. Crowfoot uncovered hundreds of fragments of beautifully carved ivory. Often these had been decorated with gold leaf or with precious stones, including lapis lazuli, The designs were of Egyptian origin and included the infant Horus, the sphinx, the lotus, and the palm tree, as well as animals and human beings. It is believed that these magnificently carved pieces of ivory were produced by Phoenician craftsmen and that they were used as inlays for thrones, couches, and other pieces of fine furniture. The foreign origin of this expensive ware probably added to Amos' sense of indignation. All of this luxury will be swept away when God visits Israel's transgressions upon her. Their expensive houses may have protected them against the extremes of climate, but they would offer no protection at all against the judgment of God.

QUESTIONS

1. Do Christians have a greater accountability than those who have not received the full revelation of God?
2. Israel was well acquainted with the examples of cause and effect given by Amos in vv. 3-6 but failed to understand the significance of Amos' appearance and message. What lessons could we draw from this passage?
3. Amos was a rustic who was called to speak to the sophisticates of Israel. He lists his credentials in vv. 7-8. Do we tend to place too much significance on proper training of ministers and teachers? Do we stress too much the idea of "meeting people where they are" with the gospel message? What are proper credentials for ministers and teachers?
4. How does God judge a country for its crime and violence? Is such judgment in evidence today?
5. Do you feel that Amos is condemning excessive wealth when he speaks about winter homes and summer homes? How would you define excessive wealth

today? In the light of extreme poverty conditions in many parts of the world, could this condemnation apply to the American standard of living? To your own standard of living?

6. Is a high standard of living a deterrent to true spirituality?

7. Do you think that there are class distinctions in our society today? If so, what are some of the dangers inherent in class distinction?

8. What are some of the status symbols among us?

9. If we live a good enough life will God reward us materially?

5
The Slow Learners

Amos 4

The Judgment of the Women of Samaria (4:1-3)

This brief oracle is addressed to the prima donnas of Samaria. Perhaps Amos had been asked to address the Mount Gerizim Garden Club! As he looked at these fat, well-to-do women, these sleek, well-fed creatures, they reminded him of a herd of fat cows from Bashan, and he told them so! Bashan was the name given to the fertile region east of the Sea of Galilee whose luxuriant pastures and fine breed of cattle had become proverbial (Deut. 32:14; Ps. 22:12; Ezek. 39:18). The Scriptures give two characteristics of the cattle of Bashan: they were fat, and they were ferocious! Both of these characteristics fitted the women of Samaria. They encouraged their husbands to deal oppressively with the poor in order that they might have an adequate supply of strong drink (v. 1).

Amos knew that a nation's character is largely determined by the quality of its womanhood. If they are cruel, or careless, or unwomanly, then the nation's well-being is threatened. The women of Samaria had made pleasure their chief goal in life. Paul's admonition to the women at Ephesus was that they remember that "she that liveth in pleasure is dead while she liveth" (I Tim. 5:6). Amos pictures the women of Samaria as driving their husbands on to more deeds of violence in order that they might drink. Just to drink would have been bad enough, for no sight could be more repulsive than that of a drunken woman. But when the money that buys the drink is obtained by the crushing of the poor, then the time for judgment is overdue.

Faced with such wanton depravity, the Lord takes an oath, swearing by His own holiness that the women of Samaria will be judged according to their deeds. For God to speak is strong enough, but for Him to speak under oath is to emphasize the immutability of His word (cf. Amos 6:8; 8:7). God has given His pledge that the guilty will not escape. God's oath based upon His holiness stands in sharp contrast to the unholy character and conduct of these women.

"Behold the days are coming upon you, when they shall take you away with hooks, even the last of you with fish hooks." According to evidence supplied by II Chronicles 33:11 and numerous Assyrian inscriptions, prisoners of war were dragged along by a rope fastened to a hook that pierced the under-lip. It has been suggested by some that the word translated "last" should be rendered "hind part" or "posterior." The resultant meaning is that the women of Samaria will be taken into captivity with hooks through their lips and fish-hooks through their posteriors. The soft living of these dainty women will come to an abrupt halt.

. The word translated "palace" (AV) or "Harmon" (RSV) is difficult to interpret. The translators of the Septuagint were baffled by this verse and their version reads: "You shall cast the Rimmon to the mountain," a translation that makes no sense at all. Duhm solved the problem by changing the word "Harmon" to read "dungheap." According to this interpretation the carcasses of these fat women will be carried out through the breaches in the walls of Samaria and thrown upon the city's dungheaps. The walls will be breached in so many places that it will not be necessary for the prisoners to be removed through the gates.

The Sin of Israel's Sanctuaries (4:4-5)

This oracle condemns the empty worship carried on at Israel's sanctuaries. Here injustice receives no reprimand, but religion as usual is carried on within sight of oppression. This message may well have been delivered at Bethel during one of the great religious festivals. In a sarcastic vein the prophet summons the people to assemble at Israel's sanctuaries, not that they might offer acceptable worship to God, but that they might add to their transgression.

> Come to Bethel, and transgress; to Gilgal, and multiply transgression; bring your sacrifices every morning, your tithes every three days; offer a sacrifice of thanksgiving of that which is leavened, and proclaim freewill offerings, publish them; for so you love to do, O people of Israel!" says the Lord God.

The prophet is attacking the scrupulously correct performance of a ritual which is divorced from right living. Religious pilgrimages usually lasted three days, during which sacrifices and tithes were offered (cf. I Sam. 1:1ff.). Amos sarcastically calls for the punctilious observance of the prescribed routine. Sacrifices are to be brought every morning and tithes at the end of three days.

Bethel seems to have been an important center for the collection of tithes. This was doubtless due to the story of Jacob's dream at Bethel and his promise to give God a tithe of all his increase (Gen. 28:18-22). What better place to present one's tithes than in this hallowed spot? To proclaim and publish freewill offerings means to make a public show of one's piety, a practice condemned by Jesus (Matt. 6:1-5). The people derived great pleasure from their religious practices—"for so you love to do, O people of Israel!" They are reminded, however, that God takes no pleasure in their worship. It is as if the prophet had said, "You have your reward."

Adam C. Welch has reminded us in *Jeremiah, His Time and His Work* that "few things determine men's attitudes on religion more clearly than the statement of what they count essential to a right relation to God." The prophets knew that elaborate ritual was no substitute for righteous living. And righteousness to them meant both a right relationship to God and a right relationship to men. Participation in worship becomes a spiritually rewarding experience only when it is a conscious and spontaneous act of faith and obedience.

God's Chastisement of Israel (4:6-12)

This section of Amos contains a list of calamities that have befallen Israel and which should have brought her to her knees in repentance. Since this has not happened, she must prepare to meet her God in judgment.

The personal pronoun in verse 6 is in the emphatic position in Hebrew, and, together with the particle "also," marks the sharp contrast between the attitude of Israel toward God, as described in verses 4-5, and God's attitude toward her. They have multiplied their gifts and sacrifices to Him, but He on His part has sent them famine, drought, crop failures, pestilence, war, and earthquake. While they seek to flatter Him and to curry His favor by offering Him expensive gifts, He chastens them with every weapon in His arsenal.

This is made more emphatic by the recurrence throughout this section of the first person pronoun.

> I have given you cleanness of teeth. . . . I have withheld the rain from you. . . . I have caused it to rain upon one city, and caused it not to rain upon another city. . . . I have smitten you with blight and mildew. . . . I have sent among you a pestilence. . . . I have slain your young men with the sword. . . . I have made the stench of your camp come up into your nostrils. . . . I have overthrown some of you as God overthrew Sodom and Gomorrah. . . .

In the final analysis, the prime mover in Israel's chastisement is neither the Assyrian conqueror nor the forces of nature, but God Himself.

The suggestion that God uses natural calamities, such as droughts and earthquakes, to punish wrongdoers raises certain questions. Snaith has observed that, curiously enough, insurance companies still refer to such calamities as "acts of God." But to what extent is one justified in using this terminology? To be sure, some of these chastisements, as, for example, war and famine, may result from "man's misguided attempts to order the affairs of this world." Here the relation is that of cause and effect. But the situation is not so simple when one considers droughts, floods, and earthquakes. May these, too, be related to man's inhumanity to man, his stupidity, his sinfulness? Is it too much to say that in a moral universe even nature itself is not neutral? Perhaps in ways beyond man's ability to determine or to comprehend there is a relation between these violent eruptions in nature and the burden of human sin (cf. Rom. 8:19-23). Recognizing such a possibility, one must beware, however, of attributing disasters to some specific act of sin or disobedience (cf. Luke 13:4-5). This is a realm of mystery, and there are many things that we do not understand. Let us admit our ignorance and acknowledge that "the secret things belong to the Lord our God" (Deut. 29:29a).

The first two chastisements mentioned are famine (v. 6) and drought (vv 7-8), the former probably caused by the latter. There are two parallel lines at the beginning of verse 6: "I gave you cleanness of teeth in all your cities, and lack of bread in all your places." This is an example of what Hebrew grammarians call synonymous parallelism, where for the sake of emphasis and clarity the thought expressed in the first line is repeated in the second. Following this principle the interpreter knows that "cleanness of teeth" means "want of bread." When men have nothing to eat, then, naturally, their teeth are going to be clean!

The drought described in verses 7-8 was caused when God withheld the rainfall three months before the harvest. In Palestine the rains come during the winter months, from around the end of October until the middle of April. The heaviest rains come at the beginning and at the end of this season, and are known in the Old Testament as the "early rains" and the "latter rains" (cf. Deut. 11:14; Jer. 5:25; Hos. 6:3). The grain harvest, which begins the latter part of April, is dependent upon adequate rainfall during the winter months. For God to withhold the rain when there were yet three months to the harvest (v. 7a) spelled crop failure and famine.

In the latter part of verse 7, the rainfall is pictured as sporadic. One city had water; another had none. One field was rained upon; another withered. The mountainous terrain of Palestine produces similar situations even today. The inhabitants of some of the drought-stricken cities staggered (a better translation than "wandered") from city to city in search of water, but were not satisfied.

Verse 9 describes crop failure due to blight and locusts. The words translated "blight and mildew" always appear together in the Scriptures (cf. Deut. 28:22; I Kings 8:37; II Chron. 6:28; Hag. 2:17). Furthermore, they are always used to describe chastisement for some act of disobedience. The word "blight" comes from the same verb root that occurs in Genesis 41:6, 23, 27, where it is rendered "blighted by the east wind." It describes, therefore, the burning up of the crops by the sirocco winds that swept in from the desert. These winds were especially fearsome and destructive. The second word, which should be seen as parallel in meaning to the first, could hardly refer to mildew. It is derived from a root meaning "to become pale" (cf. Jer. 30:6) and, therefore, describes the premature yellowing of the standing crops as a result of the scorching winds.

Verse 10 speaks of pestilence and death in the war camps of Israel. Young men die of the pestilence and fall by the sword until the stench becomes unbearable. The reference to the pestilence "after the manner of Egypt" has caused considerable discussion among commentators. The difficulty could perhaps be removed by regarding the first two clauses of the verse as another instance of Hebrew parallelism. The pestilence after the manner of Egypt is simply the slaying of the choice young men of Israel, a tragedy like that which befell the land of Egypt on the eve of the exodus.

Verse 11 refers to destruction by earthquake and fire. The prophet emphasizes the completeness of the destruction. The few who escaped were "as a brand plucked out of the burning" (cf. Zech. 3:2; Isa. 1:9).

Once again Amos mentions the possibility that a remnant will be saved from destruction. In 3:12, where the idea first appears, it is a mutilated remnant; here it is a scorched remnant.

In spite of all the evidences of divine displeasure, the people have refused to repent. Five times the Lord says, "Yet you did not return to me" (vv. 6, 8, 9, 10, 11). This five-fold repetition emphasizes not only the stubbornness of the people but also the forebearance of God. Each of the calamities had been an invitation to repentance. Through famine, drought, pestilence, war, and earthquake, God has been calling for His people to return to Him. Five times they have heard the invitation, and five times they have refused it.

Since they have refused to return to God, they have nothing to look forward to but a fearful prospect of judgment. They would not come to God for pardon, so He will come to them with punishment. This punishment will be far more dreadful than any of the previous calamities. It has been customary for verse 12 to be interpreted as a gracious invitation to life. To give it such a meaning is to ignore the context in which it stands. No one would deny that there are exhortations to repentance in the Book of Amos, but this is certainly not one of them. Israel is told to get set to meet her God, whose patience has been exhausted. To borrow a figure of speech from Hosea 13:8, He will come upon His people with the fury of a bear that has been robbed of her cubs. "Therefore thus will I do to you, O Israel." That is, the calamities just enumerated are but a sample of what is yet in store for the rebellious nation. "And because I will do this to you, prepare to meet your God, O Israel!" Amos would have agreed wholeheartedly with the statement in Hebrews 10:31: "It is a fearful thing to fall into the hands of the living God."

The First Nature Hymn (4:13)

It is generally acknowledged that this verse consists of a hymn celebrating God's glory in nature. There are three such hymns in the Book of Amos, the other two occurring in 5:8-9 and 9:5-6. There was a time when Old Testament scholars dated these hymns in the post-exilic period, primarily because of their developed doctrine of creation. This position is no longer regarded as sound since similar hymns of creation have been found in early Egyptian and Mesopotamian literature. Some have even suggested that these hymns are much older than Amos and that they were borrowed by him from an ancient cultic liturgy. There is no longer any reason to doubt the antiquity of these hymns.

Another factor to be considered in studying these hymns is the apparent lack of connection between them and the contexts in which they have been placed. In this regard they resemble the "servant poems" in Deutero-Isaiah. In the case of 4:13, however, this problem may be more apparent than real. For regardless of who may have been the original author of this hymnic portion, it appears that it was placed here to show the power and majesty of the God whom Israel must prepare to meet. The latter part of verse 12 ("because I will do this to you . . . ") may actually belong with the hymn. According to this arrangement, the hymn opens with a call for Israel to prepare for an encounter with her God, and then continues with a series of five descriptive statements depicting Israel's God as the Lord of creation. The hymn closes with a refrain which identifies this mighty

Creator by name; He is the Lord, the God of hosts. That is His name! Amen!

QUESTIONS

1. Was Amos wise in using such harsh language in addressing the elite women of Samaria? Are there times when a person has to talk tough? Why should Christians go beyond merely speaking out against social injustices?
2. Amos denounced sarcastically Israel's religious practices. How should a congregation today establish its priorities as far as its foreign and domestic mission programs, and its own edifice and furnishings are concerned?
3. How and why did the Lord chastise His people? What judgments has the Lord brought upon the world in modern times?
4. Are economic hardships and extended illness or disease indicative of God's punishment? How should Christians react to such adversity?
5. Do we recognize God the creator sufficiently? Have we become so scientifically minded that we have forgotten to praise God for His wonderful creation?

6

An Invitation to Live

Israel's Funeral Hymn (5:1-3)

These verses are written in a peculiar poetic form known as the "Qinah" meter. "Qinah" is the Hebrew word for "dirge" or "lamentation." This meter follows a 3-2 pattern, which means that the first line has three beats, the second only two, the third three, the fourth only two, and so on throughout the poem. The use of this meter produced a limping or halting effect which was quite appropriate for funeral marches or dirges. Amos is composing a funeral hymn for Israel, a nation sick beyond recovery.

The prophet calls upon the desperately ill nation to listen as he recites the lamentation that will be sung at her funeral (v. 1). She is described as a virgin who has been left lying upon the ground without strength to raise herself and with no one to lift her up (v. 2). The verb in this verse is the perfect, or completed state: so certain is the prophet that Israel will fall that he describes her fall as if it had already occurred.

The idea of a remnant comes to the fore again in verse 3. This time it is a decimated remnant; the city that musters a thousand men for battle will see only a hundred return, and the troop that marches out a hundred-strong will be reduced to ten. In the face of such devastating losses, the land will never again regain its greatness.

The Destruction of Israel's Sanctuaries (5:4-7)

In this oracle the prophet attacks Israel's time-honored sanctuaries at Bethel, Gilgal, and Beer-sheba. Gilgal was the first encampment of the Israelites west of the Jordan, and is frequently mentioned in the Old Testament as a favorite place of worship (cf. I Sam. 10:8; Hos. 4:15). Beer-sheba was also a very ancient shrine, associated with the patriarchs (cf. Gen. 21:14, 31; 26:25, 33; 46:1). Bethel and Gilgal lay within the territory of the Northern Kingdom, whereas Beer-sheba was situated some fifty miles southwest of Jerusalem in the land of Judah. This explains the phrase "cross over" in verse 5; it refers to a religious pilgrimage, a crossing over into the land of Judah to visit Beer-sheba.

To seek God may mean two different things in the Old Testament. It may mean to go to the sanctuary to sacrifice or to consult the sacred oracle (cf. Gen. 25:22; I Sam. 9:9). A second meaning is to enter into fellowship with God through love and obedience (cf. Hos. 10:12; Isa. 9:13). It is this latter meaning that is implied in the exhortation of verse 4: "For thus says the Lord to the house of Israel, 'Seek me and live.' "

When the prophet adds, "But do not seek Bethel, and do not enter into Gilgal or cross over to Beer-sheba," he is affirming that one does not have to visit a sanctuary in order to find God. In fact, the situation was such in Israel that one had best stay away from these places if he would really find God. "An attachment to bricks and mortar," writes Norman H. Snaith in *Amos, Hosea and Micah,* "is no substitute for religion." "Back to God" and "back to church" do not necessarily mean the same thing; they may even be diametrically opposed to each other.

Israel's sanctuaries are to be destroyed. Amos states this in a play on words that is difficult to reproduce in translation. The Hebrew words translated "for Gilgal shall surely go into exile" would be transliterated "*gilgal galoh yigleh*." In order to preserve the recurring sounds in the Hebrew, scholars have suggested a variety of translations. "Gilgal shall taste the gall of exile" (Smith). "Gilgal will go to the gallows" (Wellhausen). The present writer has suggested this translation to his students: "Gilgal is a gone gosling!" The second expression, "Beth-el shall come to nought," means Beth-el (house of God) will become Beth-aven (house of nothing). Bethel is actually referred to by this derisive title in Hosea 4:15. Wellhausen's translation reads: "Bethel will go to the Devil."

The following illustration, taken from an unknown source, serves well to illustrate Amos' words:

> On a certain Sunday morning the Devil passed a church and paused to listen to the songs coming from within. The congregation was singing, "Where He Leads Me I Will Follow," "I Surrender All," and "My Jesus, I Love Thee." A passerby asked the Devil why he didn't go in and disrupt the service. "Doesn't worship like this frighten you?" he asked. The Devil assured him that he wasn't at all disturbed, and as he left he was heard to say,
>
> "They're praising God on Sunday;
> They'll be all right on Monday,
> It's just a little habit they've acquired."

It is evident from verse 7 that the lavish worship carried on at Israel's sanctuaries has had no influence upon the conduct of the people. They are accused of turning justice to wormwood and of casting righteousness down to the earth. Wormwood is a bitter substance, unpleasant to the taste. The poor and oppressed of Amos' day had had to taste the bitter wormwood of injustice, meted out by "respectable" people who never missed a church service.

If we seek to apply Amos' teaching to our day, we will have to admit that a double standard of justice often prevails in the courts of our land. Rich and poor, black and white, are not treated alike. When a man's prospects for a fair trial depend upon the size of his bank account or the color of his skin, then once more justice has been turned into wormwood and righteousness has been cast down to the ground. And this is true whether the judges and jurors are "religious" men or not.

The Second Nature Hymn (5:8-9)

This is the second of the nature hymns in Amos (cf. 4:13; 9:5-6). It is generally recognized that it intrudes into the present context "in a sudden and violent way." Perhaps it was inserted at this point to emphasize the contrast between the constancy of God, as revealed in His orderly control over the forces of nature, and the inconstancy of the people of Israel.

God is pictured here as the creator and regulator of the stars, of light and darkness, and of the cycles of rainfall. It may well be that this hymn was written as a refutation of Mesopotamian religion, which deified the stars, and of Canaanite religion, which taught that Baal was the god of the storm and the giver of rain. The name of the God who does all of these things is the Lord!

According to verse 9, the God who controls the forces of nature is also in charge of the forces of destruction. The hand that moves the stars in their orbits is the same hand that smites the strongholds of Israel. This verse is poorly translated in AV; the translation of RSV is to be preferred: "who makes destruction flash forth against the strong, so that destruction comes upon the fortress." If Israel had had eyes to see, then the stars in their courses would have pointed her back to the God she had forsaken.

The Miscarriage of Justice (5:10-13)

In these verses Amos returns to his favorite theme, which is the demand for justice in the affairs of men. The prophet condemns the men of Israel for their brutal treatment of the poor. "You trample upon the poor and take from him exactions of wheat" (v. 11a). The lexicon defines an exaction as "an enforced gift taken from an inferior." In less polite language, Amos is accusing the men of Israel of highway robbery.

He further describes them as those "who afflict the righteous, who take a bribe, and turn aside the needy in the gate" (v. 12b). In ancient Israel the courtroom was the open gate at the entrance to the walled city. There the elders of the city were seated as judges to rule on cases that were brought before them (cf. v. 15; Ruth 4:1-12). In Amos' day the trials were always rigged. The judges took bribes. The word used here for bribe is derived from a root meaning "to cover." A bribe is "cover money" or "hush money." The righteous, or better, the innocent, were never acquitted in these courts but were "afflicted," that is, treated as if they were guilty. "To turn aside the needy in the gate" simply means to deny to them a fair trial. In the place where justice should have prevailed and where wrongs should have been righted, corruption and dishonesty were the order of the day.

All the while God has been a silent witness to these

transactions: "For I know how many are your transgressions, and how great are your sins . . . " (v. 12a). God's record doesn't read like the record of the court stenographer! He now sends His prophet to protest this miscarriage of justice. The prophet, however, has succeeded only in arousing the animosity of these unrighteous judges: "They hate him who reproves in the gate, and they abhor him who speaks the truth." When one dares criticize the verdicts of the judges, he is taking his life in his hands. The prudent course, therefore, would be to remain silent in such an evil time: "Therefore he who is prudent will keep silent in such a time; for it is an evil time" (v. 13). Prudence, however, is not always a virtue; the prophet who has the word of God must deliver it, even when the response is not favorable.

Amos pronounces God's judgment on Israel's unjust judges: "You have built houses of hewn stones, but you shall not dwell in them; you have planted pleasant vineyards, but you shall not drink their wine" (v. 11b). These men will be unable to enjoy the fruits of their dishonest labor, for the Judge before whom they must stand is the Lord of hosts, and He cannot be bribed.

An Invitation to Life (5:14-15)

This oracle is an elaboration of the exhortation made in verses 4 and 6: "Seek the Lord and live." In a profound way, verse 14 emphasizes the relation between religion and morality: "Seek good, and not evil, that you may live; and so the Lord, the God of hosts, will be with you, as you have said." To seek God (v. 6) and to seek good (v. 14) both lead to life. But is Amos describing two separate paths to life, or only one? Surely the latter is correct, for the prophets could not conceive of a godly man who did not live a good life.

But what is goodness? It is to "hate evil, and love good, and establish justice in the gate" (v. 15a). Goodness in Hebrew prophecy almost always has a social color. The good man is not merely the religious man, or the temperate man, or the moral man; he is the man who befriends the poor, the widow, the orphan, and the stranger; who will not take advantage of another's misfortune, but raises his voice in protest when others do so; who does everything in his power to correct oppression and to build a just and lasting society. Amos is saying, "That is good! Seek that and you shall live; ignore that, and there will be chaos and ruin."

The fruits of goodness are described in verses 14b and 15b. The first of these is life: "Seek good, and not evil, that you may live." The second is the abiding presence of God in their midst: "and so the Lord, the God of hosts, will be with you, as you have said." The third is grace and forgiveness: "it may be that the Lord, the God of hosts, will be gracious to the remnant of Joseph." Amos sees the faint possibility that a remnant of Israel may yet be spared. This is the highest point to which his optimism ever rises. Even here, however, it is not all Israel that may be saved, but only a remnant.

A Day of Lamentation (5:16-17)

In this oracle there is a prose introduction, "Therefore thus says the Lord, the God of hosts, the Lord," followed by six lines of poetry written in the Qinah meter. This is, therefore, another dirge or lamentation, written to express grief and anguish. Wailing and mourning will be heard throughout the land of Israel—in the open squares and streets of the cities, as well as in the vineyards. The mention of the latter is all the more significant since they were usually the scene of rejoicing (cf. Judg. 9:27; Isa. 16:10). Pitiful cries fill the air wherever people congregate. This is no ordinary occasion of grief, for the skilled and unskilled alike raise their voices in lamentation: the professional mourners, those "skilled in lamentation," are there, and even the farmer adds his untrained voice to theirs. Throughout the cities and the countryside there is heard the cry of despair, "Alas! Alas!"

But what is the occasion for such unbridled grief? The answer is given in verse 17b: "for I will pass through the midst of you, says the Lord." The verb translated "to pass through" is the same verb that is used in Exodus 12:12, where God declares that he will "pass through the land of Egypt" and "smite all the first-born in the land of Egypt, both man and beast." As a result of God's passing through Egypt, "there was a great cry in Egypt, for there was not a house where one was not dead" (Exod. 12:30b). On that first fateful occasion God made a distinction between the Egyptians and the Israelites; the destroyer passed over the homes of the Israelites without slaying the first-born. But now God is going to pass through the midst of Israel as He once passed through Egypt, and Israel, too, will be filled with weeping and wailing.

The Day of the Lord (5:18-20)

The day of the Lord is a term that occurs often in the Old Testament, especially in the prophetic books. It sometimes appears in abbreviated form as "the day" (Ezek. 7:12), or "that day" (Amos 8:3, 9; 9:11; Isa. 2:11-12). It is primarily the day of God's victory over His enemies, and describes the times and seasons when He intervenes in history to judge the wicked and to save the righteous. When all the references to this day are considered, it can be seen that the aspect of judgment is far more prominent than that of deliverance or salvation (cf. Zeph. 1:15).

Since there were many instances during Israel's history when God intervened to judge or to deliver, this term does not always describe the same events, but may vary in meaning from one prophet to another. Thus, in Amos the day of the Lord is related to the destruction of Israel by the Assyrians, while in Ezekiel it refers to the destruction of Jerusalem by the forces of Nebuchadnezzar (Ezek. 30:3). Both of these events were "days" of the Lord, and there were many more.

When this concept originated is not known, although it must have been prior to the time of Amos, since the men of his day seem to have been thoroughly familiar with it. Furthermore, it is evident that they regarded it as a day of deliverance for Israel, a day greatly to be desired. On this day God would deal the final blow to Israel's enemies and Israel would see the inauguration of an era of peace, prosperity, and plenty—the eighth century version of the Great Society! It is also evident that the prophet's concept of this day differed radically from that of the people. He saw it as a day of inescapable judgment and destruction.

"Woe to you who desire the day of the Lord." The verb translated "desire" is a reflexive participle, which may properly be translated as "those who desire for themselves." Actually, the men of Israel were right in supposing that on this day God would triumph over His enemies; their error was in supposing that they themselves were His friends. They looked upon this day, therefore, as a day of personal triumph.

Amos describes it as a day of unrelieved darkness and gloom (vv. 18b, 20). Terror will lurk on every hand and escape will be out of the question. It will be "as if a man fled from a lion, and a bear met him; or went into the house and leaned with his hand against the wall, and a serpent bit him" (v. 19). What a predicament for a man to be in!—chased by a lion, met by a bear, and just when he thought he had escaped into the house, a serpent came out of the wall and bit him! It should be remembered that in the days of Amos serum was unknown and snake bites were almost always fatal. Through this graphic simile, drawn from his knowledge of the desert, Amos is seeking to stress the awesome nature of the day of the Lord and the impossibility of escape. It is no wonder that he asks, "Why would you have the day of the Lord?" (v. 18b).

What Does the Lord Require? (5:21-27)

The people of Israel were certain that they knew the answer to this question. There was no difference, however, between the answer they gave and that which an Egyptian, a Canaanite, or a Babylonian would have given. In order to please God, one must provide for appropriate services to be held at His sanctuary. Naturally, these must be conducted according to a prescribed pattern. One must keep the appointed feasts and solemn assemblies (v. 21). The sacrifices, including burnt offerings, cereal offerings, and peace offerings, must be offered at designated places by duly ordained priests (v. 22). The sanctuary choirs must be well trained and provided with the finest of musical instruments (v. 23). With a service of worship like that, who could ask for anything more?

Who, indeed, but God! Listen to His opinion of Israel's stately services of worship:

I hate, I despise your feasts, and I take no delight in

your solemn assemblies. Even though you offer me your
burnt offerings and cereal offerings, I will not accept them,
and the peace offerings of your fatted beasts I will not look
upon. Take away from me the noise of your songs; to the
melody of your harps I will not listen (vv. 21-23).

Rarely in Scripture does one encounter words more
scathing than these; and they seem to be directed against
a ritual of worship that is so correct—so orthodox! To
the men of Israel the words of Amos must have sounded
utterly incredible.

What, then, does the Lord require? The answer is
given in verse 24: "But let justice roll down like waters,
and righteousness like an ever-flowing stream." Israel's
sin had choked the springs and dried up the streams of
justice and righteousness. It was a common sight in
Palestine to see fountains that had failed and streams
that had run ·dry; however, when this happened in the
spiritual realm it spelled disaster. Israel could have dispensed with her solemn assemblies, her sacrifices, and
her songs without displeasing God; but when she dispensed with justice, nothing she did could please Him.

Verse 24 might well be called the Golden Verse of
Amos, for it sounds the keynote for the entire book. One
of the best commentaries on this verse is that of John
Edgar McFayden in *A Cry for Justice: A Study in Amos*:

> These are immortal words; they express in imperishable
> form the essence of religion, the simple demands of God
> upon men. The justice, the righteousness for which Amos
> here pleads is . . . a social thing: it is a tender regard for the
> poor, hatred of the evil conditions that have dwarfed their
> lives (5:15); it is the spirit that yearns and works for the
> removal of these conditions; it is, in a word, respect for
> personality, fair play as between man and man. Let justice,
> in that sense run through society, unimpeded by avarice or
> selfishness or cruelty, let it roll on without let or hindrance
> like the waves of the sea; let it roll on unintermittently, all
> the year round, whatever be the political weather; let it roll

on "like a perennial stream" which even in the fiercest heat of summer never dries up.

In a real sense Amos was a man of one idea, and this idea had completely mastered him. He had caught a vision of a just society, a society in which religion was no longer a matter of rites and ceremonies, but where the true service of God was the service of the poor and the oppressed (cf. Isa. 58:5-12).

Such preaching as this always contains within it the seeds of revolution. The prophets saw their task not as that of defending an existing order of society but of proclaiming the kingdom of God and His righteousness. While Amos may have believed that it was normal for a community to contain both rich and poor—contrary to communism, with its myth of a classless society—he, nevertheless, did not believe that it was normal or right for the rich to oppress the poor. Furthermore, it should be noted that he derived his social concern from a strong affirmation of the sovereignty of God, and not from a denial of the existence of God, as was the case with Karl Marx. If the churches had given more attention to the preaching of prophets like Amos, perhaps the world would never have been cursed with communism. The revolutions of the nineteenth and twentieth centuries came largely because the churches of Christendom had chosen to ignore their social responsibility.

Verses 25-27 remain to be considered. This is one of the most difficult as well as one of the most debated passages in the Old Testament. Part of the difficulty lies in the fact that the different versions of the Bible are not in agreement as to how these verses should be read. It is a good exercise in textual criticism to examine the different readings found in the Hebrew, the Targum, the Greek, and in Stephen's sermon in Acts 7:42-43.

In verse 25 God directs a question to the people of Israel: "Did you bring to me sacrifices and offerings the forty years in the wilderness, O house of Israel?" The grammatical structure of this verse, in both its Hebrew and its Greek forms, demands a negative response: "No, you did not!" The two terms employed here, sacrifices and offerings, cover all types of sacrifices—animal as well as vegetable—that were offered in the pre-exilic period. This serves to emphasize the all-inclusive nature of the inquiry; it was as if God had asked, "Did you bring to me any sacrifices at all during the forty years in the wilderness, O house of Israel?"

Some have interpreted the forty years as the period of Israel's punishment after the sending out of the spies from Kadeshbarnea (Num. 14:34). Following this episode Israel was forbidden to enter Canaan until forty years has passed. Scholars who hold this view reason that Israel recognized that she had rebelled against God and that no amount of sacrifices would alter her punishment, so for forty years she refrained from offering any sacrifices at all. The chief difficulty with this view is that forty years is the customary way of describing the entire period of wilderness wanderings, from the time Israel left Egypt until she entered Canaan (cf. Exod. 16:35; Deut. 2:7; 8:2; Amos 2:10).

The crucial problem here is whether or not Israel did indeed offer sacrifices to God during the period of the wilderness wanderings. The text seems to state quite emphatically that she did not. There is apparent support for this position in Jeremiah 7:21-23:

> Thus says the Lord of hosts, the God of Israel: "Add your burnt offerings to your sacrifices, and eat the flesh. For in the day that I brought them out of the land of Egypt, I did not speak to your fathers or command them concerning burnt offerings and sacrifices. But this com-

mand I gave them, 'Obey my voice, and I will be your God, and you shall be my people; and walk in all the way that I command you, that it may be well with you' " (cf. also Isa. 1:10-17; 66:3; Hos. 6:6; Mic. 6:6-8; Ps. 50:7-15; 51:16-17).

In the light of the references cited above, many Old Testament scholars have concluded that the sacrificial system was not an integral part of Hebrew religion during the Mosaic period. J. Wellhausen is the chief advocate of this view. His position is that the sacrificial system does not date back to Moses but was taken over *en bloc* from the Canaanites after the conquest of Palestine. The prophets were opposed to it, therefore, because they regarded it as pagan in its origin and pernicious in its effects. What they wished to see accomplished, according to Wellhausen, was the abolition of the entire sacrificial system.

A more cautious position has been taken by Norman K. Gottwald:

> Whether he intends to say that sacrifice was definitely no part of the Mosaic cult or rather that there was no opportunity for it in the wilderness and thus the Hebrews got along without it, Amos certainly stresses the irrelevance of sacrifice to the main concern of religion. For him it was peripheral at best and insidiously dangerous at worst, for ritual had the habit of putting people into moral slumber so that thinking themselves fastidiously religious they do not hear the voice of Yahweh in its far-reaching demands.

There are other scholars who do not accept this evaluation of Israel's sacrificial system. The most outstanding spokesman for this group is H. H. Rowley in *The Faith of Israel:*

> It has been maintained that the sacrificial ritual of Israel was essentially of Canaanite origin. Such a view may claim some support from Amos 5:25 and Jer. 7:22, as these verses are commonly understood. ... Both these texts would seem to deny that Israel had offered sacrifice in the wilderness period. I have more than once offered my rea-

sons for dissenting from the common view. In passages of greater antiquity than the time of Amos we find references to sacrifices in the time of Moses, and if Amos and Jeremiah had wished to challenge this tradition they would have done so more directly than by a rhetorical question and a passing allusion.

What Amos was attacking, according to this view, was not the sacrificial system *per se* but sacrifice divorced from right living.

Verse 26 refers to Israel's worship of the star-gods Sakkuth and Kaiwan. The names of these two gods have been found together in at least one Assyrian text. The translation of this verse in AV—"But ye have borne the tabernacle of your Moloch and Chiun your images, the star of your god . . . "—completely misses the meaning of the Hebrew and is to be rejected in favor of RSV. Sakkuth is another name for the Assyrian wargod Adar-Melek-Saturn, also known as Ninurta. Kaiwan also is an Assyrian star-god, sometimes identified with the planet Saturn.

A crucial problem in the interpretation of verse 26 has to do with the tense of the verb—whether it is to be explained as past or as future. Since it is a form of the Hebrew perfect with the conjunction attached, it could be interpreted as either past or future, depending on the context. Since in this instance it is preceded by a perfect in verse 25, one would expect it to be translated in the past tense. This is the way it has been rendered by the Septuagint, the Targum, the New Testament (Acts 7:43), and AV. According to this translation it is not the contemporaries of Amos who are being charged with idolatry but their ancestors who are engaged in the worship of certain star-gods in the wilderness. The chief difficulty with this interpretation is that the gods referred to here are Assyrian gods and would presumably not be known in Israel until the Assyrian period—that is, until shortly before the time of Amos. They are not mentioned in any of the earlier narratives covering the period of the wilderness wanderings.

Because of this difficulty and because the verb in the following verse is translated as future, the RSV and most modern commentators prefer to render verse 26 in the future tense: "You shall take up Sakkuth your king, and Kaiwan your star-god. . . ." According to this translation Amos is declaring to the men of Israel that they will be made to carry their whole pantheon of idols with them when they are led away into captivity beyond Damascus.

The reference to the place of captivity as "beyond Damascus" is perhaps purposely vague, though it is generally conceded that Amos had in mind Assyria. This passage ends on a note of judgment, as is true of most of the passages in Amos. The words of G. E. Wright in *The Book of the Acts of God* form a fitting conclusion to Chapter 5:

> Because Israel has corrupted her common life and has violated every condition of her existence, God is now about to destroy her as a nation. And her destruction will be the first in a series of events which can be described as "the day of the Lord." That Amos should have said these words at a time of great national prosperity and triumph meant that his message was not gladly received. Nevertheless, what he had to say was at least partially verified in Israel by the destruction of the Northern Kingdom within thirty or forty years after he uttered his prophecy.

QUESTIONS

1. Discuss the concept "day of the Lord" as used in Amos 5; also in its Messianic sense.
2. Israel was guilty of corrupting worship and shaping worship activities according to her own notions. How do Christians today make this same mistake?

3. What is a "Christian" standard of living?
4. When is it wise to earn as much money as possible?
5. Is it ever right to let an aggressor take advantage of a friend, neighbor, fellow human being? What is your responsibility as a Christian in attacking social injustices prevalent today?
6. Do you believe that recent Supreme Court decisions (e.g., integration, discrimination, school busing) have helped or hindered human rights?
7. Do the poor and disadvantaged receive justice in our courts today? If not, what can/should Christians do about it?
8. In your opinion, are enough sermons devoted to the topic of social injustices? Does the church as an organization have a responsibility to go beyond preaching about injustices?

7

Confident,
Careless Citizens Condemned

Amos 6

At Ease in Zion (6:1-7)

The structure of this section is characterized by the constant recurrence of the participle with the article: "those who feel secure" (v. 1b); "those who put far away" (v. 3); "those who lie" (v. 4a); "those who stretch themselves" (v. 4b); "those who sing" (v. 5); "those who drink" (v. 6).

In these verses Amos addresses himself to the members of Israel's aristocracy, who live in luxury and imagine that they are secure from all danger. The phrase translated "the notable men of the first of the nations" means literally the "pierced" men—that is, the "marked" men, those in the upper echelons of society. They were "the favored citizens of a favored nation." To these men of distinction the house of Israel came for judgment and counsel (v. 1b). Some have detected a note of sarcasm in these words, suggesting that this is not Amos' opinion of these men but rather their own opinion of themselves.

Amos characterizes these leaders of Israel as "those who are at ease in Zion," and "who feel secure on the mountain of Samaria." Translated more literally the last clause would read: "those who trust in the mountain of Samaria." "Those who are at ease" is the rendering of the plural form of an adjective that is found only ten times in the Old Testament; the verb root from which it is derived occurs some five times. The basic meaning of the verb is to be relaxed and carefree, disdainful of all threat of harm. This can best be illustrated by reference to some of the other passages in which it, or the adjective derived from it, occurs. In Proverbs 1:33, for example, the verb is translated: "but he who listens to me [i.e., to wisdom] will dwell secure and *will be at ease*, without dread of evil." The adjectival form is found in Isaiah 32:11a: "Tremble, you women *who are at ease*, shudder, you complacent ones." Finally, in Job 12:5a, one reads: "In the thought of one *who is at ease* there is contempt for misfortune."

When these references are examined in the Hebrew they show an even more marked resemblance to Amos 6:1 than is apparent in the various translations. They serve to illustrate the complacent attitude of the men of Israel. Amos states in verse 3 that they have "put far away the evil day," which means that they have disdainfully rejected the idea that their day of reckoning may be near at hand. It is further stated (v. 3b) that they have "brought near the seat of violence." The word for seat may also be rendered "throne." According to this interpretation, Amos is saying that their arrogant attitudes and policies have resulted in the enthronement of violence in Israel.

What is the basis for such boundless optimism possessed by the leaders of Israel? Verse 1 states that they trusted in the mountain of Samaria. This may be a veiled reference to the gods of Samaria, since their abode was fixed upon the sacred mountain. More likely, however, it is a reference to the mountain upon which Samaria, the capital of Israel, was situated. This mountain was deemed to be well-nigh impregnable, and, as a matter of fact, the defenders of Samaria were able to hold out for three years against the besieging armies of Assyria before they finally surrendered in 722 B.C. This writer can testify to the feeling of awe that one has even today when he stands upon the top of this mountain amid the ruins of ancient fortresses and gazes down into the valley below. It is no wonder that the leaders of Israel trusted in the mountain of Samaria!

The reference to Zion in verse 1 has been variously interpreted. Some regard it as a later addition to the Book of Amos, placed here to make his words of condemnation apply to Jerusalem as well as to Samaria. Others see no reason why Amos himself should not have addressed both Judah and Israel; under similar circumstances the prophet Micah, while preaching to Jerusalem, referred also to Samaria (Micah 1:5-6). It may well be that this is nothing more than an example of literary parallelism, where Zion has been used in the first line to balance the reference to Samaria in the second line. The authenticity of the reference to Zion is witnessed to by all of the ancient versions.

Verse 2 presents a number of problems. Unlike the verses around it, it contains no participles, but rather a series of imperatives. The prophet commands the men of Israel to visit two cities lying to the north of Israel, Calneh and Hamath, and another lying to the south, Gath of the Philistines. He then asks, "Are they better than these kingdoms? Or is their territory greater than your territory?" The Prophet seems to be saying that from north to south there are no kingdoms superior to Judah and Israel in quality or in size, excluding, of course, Egypt and Assyria. The implied conclusion is that the favored position of Judah and Israel makes their sin all the more serious.

The three cities referred to in this verse were destroyed by the Assyrians during the period from 720 to 711 B.C. In view of this fact many recent commentators have emended the verse to read: "Are you (Israel) better than these kingdoms, or is your territory greater than theirs?" In other words, if these kingdoms did not escape the wrath of the Assyrians, why do you imagine that you will escape?

The chief objection to this emendation—apart from the fact that it lacks support in any of the ancient versions—is that Amos could not have spoken these words, since his ministry had ended long before these cities were destroyed. Furthermore, the problem is not solved by suggesting that this was added later by a disciple of Amos, for it would still have been meaningless if addressed to Samaria after 721 B.C. These suggested solutions create more problems than they solve. It is preferable to leave the verse as it is, even though its meaning is somewhat obscure.

Verses 4-6 describe the luxury and self-indulgence of the men of Israel. They lie upon beds of ivory and sprawl upon their couches while they eat. This is the first time Scripture refers to men reclining at meals; heretofore they had eaten in a sitting position (cf. Judg. 19:6; I Sam. 20:5, 25; II Kings 4:10). Amos regarded this innovation as a sign of self-indulgence and lewdness. They ate only the choicest meats—tender mutton and high grade veal. Since most Israelites could rarely afford to include meat in their diet, Amos regarded this luxury as wanton and inexcusable.

They sang idle songs to the random strumming of their harps; each one tried to be a little David. Since ordinary cups were too small for them, they drank wine from bowls (v. 6). The word translated "bowls" is one that usually describes the sacred vessels reserved for the temple services (cf. Exod. 27:3; Num. 7:13f.; I Kings 7:40). The ancient rabbis interpreted this verse to mean that the men of Israel were profaning these sacred vessels by using them in their feasts. There is a remarkable similarity between the behavior of these men and that of King Belshazzar who, while drinking wine from the temple vessels, saw the handwriting on the wall (Dan. 5).

And so the men of Israel reveled in their luxury—ivory beds, quality meats, private orchestras, wine, and the most expensive cosmetics. They were well-adjusted members of an affluent society, possessing both wealth and the leisure to enjoy it. Their sin was the sin described in Jesus' parable of the rich man and Lazarus: engrossed in the spending of their wealth, they were totally unconcerned for the less fortunate members of society. In the words of Amos, they were not grieved over the ruin of Joseph. The word translated "ruin" is sometimes rendered "destruction" (Prov. 16:18), "hurt" (Jer. 6:14), "bruise" (Jer. 30:12), or "affliction" (Jer. 30:15). It conveys the idea of someone who has been mortally wounded beyond all hope of recovery. Perhaps in the mention of the ruin of Joseph there is an allusion to the heartless behavior of the brothers of Joseph, who sold him into slavery and brought his blood-stained coat in order to deceive their father. Here, of course, Joseph stands for all the tribes of Israel.

Amos pronounces judgment upon Israel's aristocrats in verse 7. The words of this verse have a peculiar force and abruptness in the Hebrew. Even the word "therefore" with which the verse begins should not be overlooked; as McFadyen has observed, "those who have breathed the atmosphere of Amos learn to tremble when he utters his 'therefore,' for they know that something terrible is coming." Israel's first families will be the first to go into captivity. These who have made themselves conspicuous by their extravagance will soon be conspicuous by their absence. Their revelry will cease and a strange quietness will settle over the land.

How Are the Proud Abased! (6:8-11)

This passage begins with God taking an oath. Swearing by Himself He says, "I abhor the pride of Jacob, and hate his strongholds; and I will deliver up the city and all that is in it." Jacob is synonymous with Israel, since Jacob's name was changed to Israel after he had wrestled all night with a man at the ford of the Jabbok (Gen. 32:24-28). The "pride of Jacob" probably has reference to that in which Jacob takes pride, or, in other words, to that in which he places his confidence. In this instance it seems to stand for Samaria with its strong fortifications. God makes it clear that Jacob's trust has been misplaced; the city and all that is in it will be delivered up to destruction.

There are others who interpret the pride of Jacob as the arrogant self-sufficiency of the tribes of Israel. Israel has shown herself to be the descendant of Jacob—Jacob the deceiver, the supplanter. Why then should she be proud? It is a strange fact of human experience that men often view their vices as their virtues. Snaith has pointed out that the word "pride" appears in the Septuagint as *hubris,* a word which he defines as "the insolence of a man who thinks himself equal to God."

According to verses 9 and 10, the inhabitants of the Northern Kingdom will be wiped out by war and pestilence. If there are ten men left in a household, they shall die (v. 9; cf. 5:3). Verse 10 is somewhat obscure but scholars are agreed as to its general meaning. In the pestilence that will sweep across the land there will be so many victims that normal burial practices will have to be set aside and the survivors will resort to the unusual procedure of burning the corpses. When the relative of a deceased man enters his house to take out his body to be burned, he discovers that there is a lone survivor, hidden in some far corner of the house. When the relative calls out to him, he responds with a Hebrew interjection translated "Hush!" and then adds, "We must not mention the name of the Lord." These men have profaned the name of God in the past but now they dare not pronounce it, lest it loosen some fresh avalanche of His wrath. It is significant that even to this day an orthodox Jew will not pronounce the covenant name of Israel's God.

Not only will the dead be in every house but the houses themselves will be smitten into fragments (v. 11). The same fate will befall great and small houses.

The Final Chapter in a Sordid History (6:12-14)

Verse 12 asks two questions which demand a negative answer: "Do horses run upon rocks? Does one plow with oxen?" The translation given here is a literal rendering of the Hebrew. If the second of these questions is examined, however, it will readily be seen that a negative answer does not make sense; men *do* plow with oxen. AV sought to remove this difficulty by inserting the italicized word "there" in its translation: "will one plow *there* [i.e., on the rocks] with oxen?"

Most modern translators emend this question to read, "Will one plow the sea with oxen?" This is a simple emendation that effects no changes in the consonants of the Hebrew; it, therefore, has much to commend it. The men of Israel would readily see the absurdity of imagining that someone would run horses upon the rocks or plow the sea with oxen. It is equally absurd for Israel to pervert justice and then to exult in her military prowess.

This is probably the sense of verse 13, as it has been translated in RSV: "you who rejoice in Lo-debar, who say, 'Have we not by our own strength taken Karnaim for ourselves?'" Lo-debar and Karnaim were insignificant villages that lay east of the Jordan, and it is supposed that Jeroboam II had captured them in his campaigns against the Syrians. They were probably selected by the prophet because of the suggestiveness of their names, Lo-debar meaning "a no-thing" and Karnaim "a pair of horns," that is, a symbol of power. The men of Israel were actually boasting of their successful exploits on the field of battle. No doubt they regarded the capture of these small villages as but the prelude to greater exploits. To do this was utter folly for at that very moment God was raising up an enemy who would lay waste the country from one end to the other. It is on this somber note that the second section of Amos comes to a close.

QUESTIONS

1. The phrase, "Woe to them that are at ease in Zion" was addressed to the aristocracy living in luxury in Israel's capital city. Discuss ways in which this warning might apply today to lovers of luxury. Could this warning be applied to Christians also? How?
2. What dangers are inherent in luxurious living?
3. What portion of our money/luxuries may we keep for ourselves?

4. When does party-going, banqueting, eating well become wrong?
5. Do people repent readily when God's judgments come, or do they harden themselves still more?

8
A Horde of Locusts
and a Burning World

Amos 7:1-6

These chapter describe the visions which God gave to Amos foretelling pestilence, earthquake, famine and locusts, all stern reminders to the people that they should return to God before the greatest calamity of all—captivity—overtakes them. A literary framework is evident in 7:1, 4, 7, and 8:1, where the clause, "Thus the Lord God [or, He] showed me," occurs.

The first three visions are found in 7:1-9, and are followed by the historical section (7:10-17) describing Amaziah's response to Amos' preaching and his attempt to squelch the prophet and to force him to return to Judah. In this encounter the prophet refused to be silenced, and justified his presence in Bethel by referring to the divine call that had come to him. He then proceeded to tell how the approaching disaster would affect the household of the high priest.

The fourth vision (8:1-3) likens Israel to a basket of summer fruit, ripe for the eating. The time of mercy had ended and the end of Israel was in sight. Following this vision there is a further description of the sins which have justified such harsh action on the part of God.

The fifth and final vision (9:1-4) tells of the smiting of the sanctuary and of the futility of trying to flee from the judgment that is coming. The last of the nature hymns appears in 9:5-6. The last oracle of Amos

(9:7-10) combats the false notion that God's election of Israel will exempt her from judgment. Evil will relentlessly pursue the sinners and will overtake even those who regard themselves as immune to it.

Chapter 9 concludes with an epilogue of hope (vv. 11-15), in which is painted a glorious picture of the Day of the Lord, when Israel would be brought back from exile and her fertile soil would yield bumper crops. For reasons that will be discussed below, this concluding epilogue is generally regarded as a later addition to the Book of Amos.

The First Vision (7:1-3)

It has been suggested that the three visions in 7:1-9 form the substance of a sermon which Amos preached at Bethel and which culminated in his encounter with the priest Amaziah (7:10-17). This suggests that these three visions were revealed to Amos on the same occasion and that they, therefore, form a unity. It is far more likely that they came to Amos at different times over a period of several months and that each one was a complete sermon in itself. It was only when the prophet's messages were collected in written form that these visions were grouped together as we now have them.

Another suggestion is that these visions are to be dated at the beginning of the prophet's ministry and that they constitute his call and preparation for his mission. Another authority thinks it possible that this cycle of visions—which reflects spring (7:1-3), summer (7:4-6), and fall (8:1-3)—may indicate that the prophet's ministry extended over a period of several months. If this interpretation is correct, then it is reasonable to suppose that Amos had traveled extensively, delivering his messages in the various towns and villages of Israel. As his ministry unfolded he became increasingly convinced that Israel was past redemption and that judgment was inevitable. This can be seen not only in the visions but also in the oracles in chapters 1–6.

The vision in 7:1-3 is set in the spring of the year after the "latter rains" of April (cf. 4:7) had caused the "latter growth" of grass. After this there would not be another growth of grass sufficient for mowing until the "early rains" came in October. This made the plague of locusts described here all the more serious. The reference to the "king's mowings" has been variously interpreted. It is usually interpreted as referring to the king's right to the first mowing, a sort of royal levy on the land, after which the second growth went to the tenants of the land. Others prefer the translation, "after the king's shearings," a translation which is certainly permissible from the standpoint of the Hebrew. According to this translation the passage makes no reference to a royal levy on the land but simply dates this vision in the spring of the year, immediately after the royal flocks had been sheared (cf. II Sam. 13:23).

The vision is of a devouring plague of locusts that threatens to destroy the latter growth of grass. It must be remembered that there were no insecticides in the days of Amos and the defenseless farmers were entirely at the mercy of the swarms of locusts. Upon seeing the danger that threatens Jacob, the prophet intercedes for him: "O Lord God, forgive, I beseech thee! How can Jacob stand? He is so small!" It is important to remember that in the Old Testament the ministry of intercession is performed not so much by the priest as by the prophet (cf. Gen. 20:7). When one is tempted to think of Amos as a prophet of doom who had little concern for those to whom he preached, he should remember these earnest prayers of intercession. Amos recognized that he had no right to preach to people unless he had prayed for them.

The ministry of intercession is much more prominent in the Bible than it is in the lives of modern Christians. The great intercessors include Abraham, Moses, Samuel, Isaiah, Job, and Amos. Christ prayed for His enemies, and it is stated that "he is able also to save them to the uttermost that come unto God by him, seeing he ever liveth to make intercession for them" (Heb. 7:25, AV).

Our world is filled with bewildered men and women who desperately need an intercessor. Why, then, is so little emphasis placed upon intercessory prayer? Perhaps the reason is that intercessory prayer costs so much, for it involves more than an attitude of benevolence. Although it includes prayer, it involves far more than prayer. Intercession really involves a way of life, so that one cannot pray intercessory prayers unless he is living an intercessory life. The ministry of intercession can never be performed behind cloistered walls, for if we would truly pray for the poor, we must be ready to identify with them in their poverty; if we would pray for the lost, we must be out seeking them; if we would pray for missions, we must be ready to go wherever God calls us. If this is not so, then our prayer has become a sham and a pretense.

After Amos had prayed for Jacob it is stated that the Lord repented concerning the locusts. "To repent" comes from a verb meaning "to change the mind." This verse teaches that God's purposes are always flexible, and that He may change His course of action whenever the changed situation warrants it. This verb always has emotional overtones, either of joy or of sorrow. God

103

may change His mind joyfully, as in this instance, or sorrowfully, as in the days of Noah, when it grieved Him that He had made man (Gen. 6:6). Originally this verb was used to describe heavy breathing, such as the labored breathing of a horse after a hard drive. It always retained something of this meaning even after it was applied to men and to God. When one repents he either sighs within himself, expressing sorrow, or heaves a sigh of relief, expressing joy. But while this verb may express either sorrow or comfort, the comfort is always that which emerges out of sorrow. God "changes His mind" in response to the prophet's prayer, not reluctantly, but with a sense of relief. To punish is always His strange work, and to pardon is His delight (cf. Isa. 28:21).

The Second Vision (7:4-6)

Once again the prophet is shown a vision of destruction and once again he is effective in his intercession on behalf of Jacob.

This vision suggests the summertime, when the land was being burned by the sun. The Hebrews thought of the earth as resting upon a vast subterranean ocean known as "the great deep." This ocean was regarded as the source of earth's springs, fountains, and rivers, and even of the rainfall. As the sun blazed in the sky, fountains and streams stopped flowing, giving the impression that the great deep itself had been dried up. The whole universe had become dehydrated and even the earth seemed to be on fire. In alarm the prophet cried out to God and disaster was averted.

QUESTIONS

1. What does it mean that the Lord was forming locusts?

Was this a type of insect not known in the world before?

2. Does Amos pray only that the plague may be averted, or is there a greater depth to his pleas? Upon what basis can the Lord prevent the destruction pictured in the vision?

3. Discuss the place and value of intercessory prayer. Is repentance and a pleading upon God's mercy sufficiently emphasized in our day?

4. Does the Lord's repenting, even in appearance, show His love or His wrath? Does the Lord's mercy, and compassion outshine His justice and anger? Which should we emphasize most?

5. Discuss "fire," "the great deep," and "the land." What are the possible meanings of these terms as given in this context?

6. Are natural catastrophies still used by God in judgment?

9
The Plumb Line

Amos 7:7-9

The Third Vision (7:7-9)

Amos saw the Lord standing beside a wall built with a plumb line and having a plumb line in His hand. Stone walls are a common sight in Palestine, especially where they have been built to terrace the hillsides. Stones lie scattered over the face of the earth in such abundance that they have to be cleared away before the fields can be cultivated. The Talmud contains a legend relating how at creation God sent Gabriel with a sack of stones to be scattered over all the earth, but while he was passing over Palestine the sack burst and all the stones spilled out!

Stone walls, built with little or no mortar, would slowly shift and settle until they were badly out of line. Since it was dangerous to leave such walls standing, they had to be demolished or else rebuilt.

In this vision Amos sees the Lord standing beside a wall built with a plumb line (literally, "a wall of a plumb line"). This indicates that the wall had been built straight, but was now off-center. The Lord had in His hand a plumb line with which He was testing the wall. He was doing this, not because He needed proof that the wall was crooked, but in order to convince the prophet that it was crooked and needed to be demolished.

God is showing Amos why Israel must be punished. In verse 8 He states that He is setting a plumb line in the midst of the house of Israel. There is a sense in which the ministry of Amos was a plumb line with which God measured and tested His people. Among those whom He checked and found to be crooked were the women of Samaria (4:1-3), the idle rich (6:4-7), the judges (5:10-13), the merchants (8:4-7), and, above all, the priests (7:10-17).

What Amos saw convinced him that God was justified in condemning Israel. In the first two visions he had interceded for Israel, but there is no further intercession after this vision. Verse 9 is God's declaration of war against His people: "The high places of Isaac shall be made desolate, and the sanctuaries of Israel shall be laid waste, and I will rise against the house of Jeroboam with the sword."

QUESTIONS

1. How does the third vision differ from the first two?
2. Why, do you suppose, did Amos not offer an intercessory prayer after seeing this vision?
3. In this vision the Lord pronounces judgment on the state. Do you feel that today's national leaders tend to give only lip service to God?
4. What responsibilities do Christians have in the area of politics and political issues? Should we have a Christian political party?
5. Should a church openly support a candidate or a political issue? Should a pastor run for public office?
6. The Lord pronounced judgment on the church also. How can the church today guard gainst the practice of cold, formal religion? What can an individual do?

7. The church was also indicted for cold, heartless materialism. Is this present in our churches today? If so, what can be done to combat it?
8. Do you think that God puts His plumb line to the church today and finds it crooked? If so, where is it out of line?

10
A Liberal and
a Conservative Clash

Amos 7:10-17

The Prophet and the Priest (7:10-17)

The record of Amos' encounter with Amaziah has been placed between the third and fourth visions, perhaps because of the reference to King Jeroboam in 7:9. This is one of the most dramatic scenes in the Bible, and it has been compared with the encounter between Jesus and Caiaphas. Claus Westermann in *A Thousand Years and a Day* has given a vivid description of the conflict between the prophet and the priest, whom he describes as:

> . . . two men who both speak and act on the orders of God, the God of Israel, and who both wish to serve their country. We must picture the conversation taking place in public. It must have happened in front of witnesses. The men of Israel saw before them two representatives of God, standing against each other. The one spoke by right of his office and on the orders of the divinely anointed king. The other spoke in the name of God without any badge of authority, without any official position and without any authority behind him. And he declared God's judgment to the divinely anointed king, to the ecclesiastically appointed priest: destruction, disgrace. What a heavy demand this scene must have made on the witnesses!

The priest, backed by the power of the state, seeks to silence the prophet of God. Prior to this encounter he had already sent word to the king accusing Amos of sedition:

> Amos has conspired against you in the midst of the
> house of Israel; the land is not able to bear all his words.
> For thus Amos has said, "Jeroboam shall die by the sword,
> and Israel must go into exile away from his land."

Amaziah quoted Amos correctly—this is precisely what the prophet had been saying—but he completely misjudged his motives and his intentions. He supposed that Amos was attempting to initiate a revolt and to remove Jeroboam from the throne. Little did he understand that the real conspirator against Israel was God Himself!

"And Amaziah said to Amos, 'O seer, go, flee away to the land of Judah, and eat bread there, and prophesy there; but never again prophesy at Bethel, for it is the king's sanctuary, and it is a temple of the kingdom'" (vv. 12-13). Seer is an older term for prophet (cf. I. Sam. 9:9), and Amaziah probably used it to show his contempt for Amos. It is ironic that one who was so blind should contemptuously refer to the prophet as seer; in so doing he expressed a deeper truth than he realized. The priest admonished the prophet to go preach for his bread in Judah, insinuating that the prophet's motives were purely mercenary. By his words he judged himself rather than the prophet. Amos is told that Bethel is off limits to peripatetic prophets, since it is the king's private sanctuary and the official temple. The time had come when the word of God was no longer tolerated, not even in the house of God.

Amos' response to Amaziah is sharp and to the point:

> "I am no prophet, nor a prophet's son; but I am a
> herdsman, and a dresser of sycamore trees, and the Lord
> took me from following the flock, and the Lord said to me,
> 'Go, prophesy to my people Israel.' Now therefore hear the
> word of the Lord" (vv. 14-16a).

A literal translation of verse 14 would read: "No prophet I, and no son of a prophet I; but a herdsman I, and a dresser of sycamores." There is no verb in the Hebrew, so that the appropriate form of the verb "to be" has to be supplied by the translator. Unfortunately, however, translators are not able to agree upon whether this should be the past tense, "I was," or the present tense, "I am."

The translators of RSV, quoted above, have preferred the present tense. According to this interpretation, Amos denies that he is a prophet or a son of a prophet. "Son of a prophet" does not refer to one whose father was a prophet but to one who belonged to a prophetic guild, known in the Old Testament as the sons of the prophets (cf. I. Sam. 10:5; I Kings 22:10-12; II Kings 4:38). Amos declares that he does not need to preach for his bread, for his income is provided by his flocks and his fig trees.

According to this line of reasoning Amos completely rejected the title of prophet and would not have it applied to himself. However, if one accepts this interpretation, he must find a plausible explanation for such passages as 2:11; 3:8; and 7:15. These passages seem to indicate that prophets ranked high in the estimation of Amos and that he did not hesitate to accept a prophetic role and to enter upon the prophetic ministry, when he felt that God had called him to do so. In other words, all of the evidence indicates that Amos was called to be a prophet, that he functioned as a prophet, and that he was known as a prophet.

In the face of this evidence there are many who prefer to translate verse 14 in the past tense: "I was no prophet, neither was I a son of a prophet; but I was a herdsman, and a dresser of sycamore trees; and the Lord took me from following the flock. . . ." According to

this translation, Amos is not denying that he is a prophet, but is making it clear that he did not choose this
office for himself.

The way to a deeper understanding of this verse has
been indicated by Watts. When 7:14ff. is studied closely,
three substantives stand out—"I," "the Lord," and
"thou." The point at issue here is the question of
authority. Who has the authority to tell Amos where he
should prophesy? Obviously, Amaziah believed that this
authority belonged to him as the priest of Bethel. Amos
in turn challenges Amaziah's right to interfere with him
when his orders have come from no less an authority
than the Lord God Himself. Amaziah, therefore, has no
right to interfere with one whom God has called and
commissioned to be a prophet to Israel. The fact that he
has attempted to do so can only mean that swift judgment will come upon him and his household.

The normal word order in a Hebrew sentence is verb,
subject, and direct object. Whenever this order is altered,
it is for the purpose of emphasis. Such is the case in
verse 17. In each of the five clauses in this verse the
subject is placed first in order that it might be emphasized. "*Your wife. . . , your sons. . . , your daughters. . . ,
your land. . . , you yourself. . . , and Israel. . . . Everything* you hold dear will soon be wiped out." Amaziah's
wife would be raped, his children slain, his property
confiscated, and he would be carried off to die in a
strange and foreign land. Thus spoke the prophet to the
priest, and the priest answered not a word!

QUESTIONS

1. Do you think that Amaziah was offended most by
   Amos' character and lack of credentials or his message?

2. Should a Christian try to be popular? May we be indifferent to public opinion? Do you think that a popular minister is more effective than one who is unpopular?

3. Do you think that God's prophets of today are honored and listened to as they should be?

4. What is wrong with human judgments on any level— either that of our enemies, our friends, or ourselves? Can one person really judge another?

5. What should be the Christian reaction to unjust criticism?

6. Do you think we would be better Christians if we had to endure more scorn and ridicule from non-Christians?

7. In verses 16 and 17 it might be said that Israel had reached the point of no return. Would this be an appropriate assessment of world conditions today? Why, or why not?

11
No Word from God

The Fourth Vision (8:1-3)

This vision announces the end of the covenant relationship and of Israel's status as the people of God. One
is struck by the note of finality that is sounded in these
words. Amos received this vision in the fall of the year at
the end of the long hot summer. Watts has given a vivid
description of the scene:

> The fruit of trees hardy enough to survive the heat had
> ripened and been gathered, and now the bare trees stood
> out against the stark brown of the landscape. All nature and
> all people yearned for the coming rains which the fall
> equinox should bring with refreshing cool, reviving mois-
> ture, and joyful entry into another year.

It is not surprising that the Israelites chose the fall
equinox (October-November) as the beginning of the
New Year, for it was then that the life-giving rains
returned to water the earth.

Verse 2 contains a play on words. Amos sees a basket
of summer fruit (Hebrew: *qayits*) and God tells him the
end (*qets*) has come upon His people Israel. Some have
tried to preserve this play on words by saying that the
fall of the year reminded the prophet of the fall of
Israel. It was not only the end of summer but also the
end of Israel. This year the refreshing rains will not
return after the summer, and there will be no renewal

for Israel. One is reminded of the words of Jeremiah 8:20: "The harvest is past, the summer is ended, and we are not saved."

It has been suggested that Amos preached this sermon when the men of Israel had assembled at Bethel to celebrate the New Year Festival. This suggestion receives support from the reference to the songs of the temple in verse 3. This would certainly have been a dramatic setting for such a sermon. While all Israel looked for a new beginning, the prophet went up and down the streets, saying, "This is the end! This is the end!"

In verse 3 one hears wailing coming from the temple, and sees the slain on every hand. This is the death rattle of a dying nation, and it is followed by an awful silence. The last line in verse 3 should be translated: "In every place he has cast out!—Hush!" (cf. 6:10).

Israel's Burden of Guilt (8:4-14)

This section repeats some of the charges made against Israel in Chapter 2—6, adding to these its own description of the impending doom. Verses 4-6 describe the insatiable greed of the merchants of Israel, to whom the days set aside for worship—the new moon and the sabbath—were bothersome interruptions to their profit making.

> Hear this, you who trample upon the needy, and bring the poor of the land to an end, saying, "When will the new moon be over, that we may sell grain? And the sabbath, that we may offer wheat for sale, that we may make the ephah small and the shekel great, and deal deceitfully with false balances, that we may buy the poor for silver and the needy for a pair of sandals, and sell the refuse of the wheat?"

Commenting on the relationship between Sabbath keeping and concern for the welfare of others, McFadyen has written:

> It is very significant that the men who do these wicked
> things sit loose on the obligations of the Sabbath day.
> Religion is a restraining as well as an inspiring force. Their
> barefaced disregard of the decencies of trade is largely the
> result of their indifference to religion; having no fear of
> God, they have no regard for man. The Sabbath-hating and
> the swindling go together. It is no accident that those who
> do not love the Sabbath cheat on Monday: they rob God
> and their own souls one day, and their neighbor the next.
> To be irreligious is to be antisocial; to be religious, in the
> sense demanded by Hebrew prophecy, is to be social. . . .

George Adam Smith in his treatment of this passage
has emphasized another truth that is often overlooked:

> As in every other relevant passage of the Old Testament,
> we have the interest of the Sabbath bound up in the same
> cause with the interests of the poor. The Fourth Command-
> ment enforces the day of rest on behalf of the servants and
> bondsmen. . . . The interests of the Sabbath are the in-
> terests of the poor: the enemies of the Sabbath are the
> enemies of the poor. And all this illustrates our Saviour's
> saying, that *the Sabbath was made for man.*

These merchants had adopted policies that in the end
would lead to the extinction of the poor. When they
offered their wheat for sale, they made the ephah small
and the shekel great. The ephah was a container in which
the merchants measured out the amount of grain which
the customer wished to buy. It normally held about
eight gallons, but these merchants had made it smaller
than the norm, thus giving their customers short meas-
ure. When the customer paid for his purchase, he had to
weigh out an amount of silver equal to the purchase
price. This was done by means of a balance, with the
merchant placing a bar of silver on one side of the
balance and the customer matching it with the same
amount on the opposite side. When the scales balanced
the customer knew that he had paid the price agreed

upon. The only difficulty was that these merchants had made their shekel, a bar of silver estimated to be worth about sixty cents, heavier than the norm, thus over-charging the customer.

Not content with such price-gouging, these merchants further increased their profits by selling the refuse and calling it wheat. The poor paid exorbitant prices only to discover later that they had purchased trash instead of bread. It was not uncommon for them to be reduced to such straits that they were forced to sell themselves into slavery for the paltry price of a pair of sandals. In the light of these practices one understands why Amos addressed the merchants of those "who trample upon the needy and bring the poor of the land to an end."

One is reminded by this passage of the way in which modern loan companies often take advantage of the man who is a poor credit risk by charging him exorbitant rates of interest. Landowners have also been known to keep their tenants in a permanent state of poverty by furnishing them all their supplies and charging them whatever they deemed fit. Not too many years past coal miners were exploited in a similar fashion by being required to make all their purchases at the "company store." Equally repulsive are such practices as price-fixing, improper labeling, and false advertising, which are all too common in our day. A nation's life depends upon commerce, but as McFadyen has pointed out:

> . . . . this is commercialism, the small, mean trading spir-it, which cares nothing for religion, nothing for art or music, nothing for anything but the endless making of money, and regards every hour as lost that is not devoted to that end. If that were all, it would be contemptible enough, but this passion for money was so keen that it refused to be satisfied in honest ways.

God solemnly vows that He will forget none of their

wicked deeds (v. 7). Verse 8 suggests the thought of an earthquake, not simply a momentary tremor but a prolonged shaking that continues like the rising and receding of the waters of the Nile, a cycle that lasts approximately two months.

The day referred to in verses 9, 10, 11, and 13 is the day of the Lord (cf. 5:18-20). Amos describes this day as a day of darkness (v. 9), of bitter grief (v. 10), of famine (vv. 11, 12), and of thirst (vv. 13, 14). The mourning will be as the mourning over the death of an only son, the bitterest form of grief imaginable in ancient Israel (cf. Jer. 6:26; Zech. 12:10).

Amos had spoken earlier of cleanness of teeth and want of bread in the cities of Israel (4:6); now, however, he describes a famine of much more serious proportions, a famine of hearing the words of the Lord (vv. 11, 12). Previously the men of Israel had despised the word of the Lord and had attempted to silence His prophets (2:12; 7:12, 13), but now they run from one end of the land to the other seeking a word from the Lord. They are ready to listen now, if only He would speak. But God remains silent and His words are heard no more in Israel. This is the end of prophecy; but it is more than this. It is the end of the covenant; God will no longer communicate His will to Israel.

Richard S. Cripps has observed in *A Critical and Exegetical Commentary on the Book of Amos* that there is a disturbing parallel between Amos' day and our own:

> Is not the plight of the world today due to "*a famine, not a famine of bread, nor a thirst for water, but of hearing the word of the LORD?*" It is not due to a lack of God-sent messengers, but to the *total indifference* of men and women to the living word of the living God which is proclaimed in the churches and which could be read and assimilated by all.

In that day fair virgins and strong young men will faint for thirst. These are the ones who have forsaken God and have sworn allegiance to Ashimah of Samaria. This is a better translation than "the sin of Samaria." Ashimah was a goddess known to have been worshiped by the men of Hamath (II Kings 17:30), and also by the community of Jewish exiles living at Elephantine in Egypt in the fifth century B.C. (cf. Jer. 44:18-19). There are two additional oaths in this verse, although this is not evident in the translation of AV; the men of Israel have sworn by the god of Dan and by the "way of Beer-sheba." This last phrase may refer to the road which pilgrims followed when en route to the shrine at Beer-sheba. The Septuagint suggests an alternate reading which involves the changing of only one consonant in Hebrew: "as thy god lives, O Beer-sheba." Dan and Beer-sheba are mentioned together because of their geographical location. Dan was the northernmost Israelite town and Beer-sheba lay on the southern border of Judah. The prophet is saying that idolatry is rampant from one end of the land to the other, "from Dan to Beer-sheba."

Those who have participated in such idolatrous worship will faint for thirst; they will fall down, never to rise again (v. 14). There is a marked contrast between these verses and the promise contained in Isaiah 40:30-31:

> Even youths shall faint and be weary, and young men shall fall exhausted; but they who wait for the Lord shall renew their strength, they shall mount up with wings like eagles, they shall run and not be weary, they shall walk and not faint.

How different the history of Israel would have been if her people had learned to wait upon the Lord!

QUESTIONS

1. How serious are social sins, that is, sins against our fellowmen? Why, do you suppose, was the list of these sins repeated in the fourth vision?

2. Can a person be a worshiper and still be guilty of these sins?

3. Do businessmen today try to get away with "making the ephah small" and "falsifying the balances by deceit"? If so, what can you as an individual do about it? Why should Christians be concerned with business ethics?

4. Are our labor unions a remedy for social ills? What contributions do they make?

5. Did God's judgment actually fall on Israel?

6. What was the famine of the Word? How did the people react to it? Is there a famine of the Word today?

7. Discuss the meaning of "Man shall not live by bread alone." Are we trying to do just that today? If so, how would you remedy this situation?

12
Holocaust Ahead

Amos 9:1-10

The Fifth Vision (9:1-4)

This final vision tells of the smiting of the sanctuary and of the futility of trying to hide from the Lord. Verse 1 speaks of the thresholds shaking and crashing down upon the heads of the people. Most commentators interpret this as a reference to destruction by an earthquake, perhaps the same earthquake referred to in Amos 1:1. The capitals supporting the roof of the temple are smitten and the building collapses upon the heads of the assembled worshipers. One is reminded of how Samson pulled down the temple of Dagon on the heads of the Philistines (Judg. 16:23-30).

Where this destruction occurred is not clear from the text; perhaps it was at Bethel. The significance of this vision has been described by McFadyen:

> It is a vision of truly titanic power. In the temple, whose courts were crowded with infatuated worshipers, Amos saw the Lord standing beside the altar—ominous sight: for the people who there, of all places, must have felt most secure, had denied Him the service for which He supremely cared—the service of an honourable public and private life, gentle and just in all its relations; and beside the altar, reeking with their foolish sacrifices, stands the mighty God whom they have insulted, ready to destroy them. Suddenly across the crowded courts rings out the dreadful word *Smite*, addressed by the Lord to some unseen angelic minister of vengeance.

When this holocaust comes no one will be allowed to escape. If, by chance, one should attempt to hide from God's wrath, he will be discovered and slain. The prophet mentions all the places where one might hope to hide from God, only to declare that in all these places God has His avenging ministers. Sheol below and heaven above, both inaccessible to living men, will provide no refuge to the fugitive (v. 2). Even if one should succeed in reaching either of these places, he would still not be beyond the reach of God. Carmel is mentioned as a possible hiding-place, because of its heavy forests and numerous caves (v. 3a); but God will lead a searching party into Carmel to find those who hide there. Even the sea will not cover them, for there the avenging God has His agent the serpent (v. 3b; cf. Gen. 1:21; Job 41:1; Isa. 27:1). And if an enemy comes and takes the Israelites into captivity to a foreign land, even there the sword will pursue and slay them (v. 4a). The final clause in verse 4 usually means to watch over one for his protection and well-being (cf. Jer. 24:6); here, however, it means that God will fix His withering gaze upon Israel until she is destroyed. The author of Psalm 139 gives a similar description of God's inscrutable understanding of his ways, which was to him a source of comfort and strength; to Israel, however, it will be a source of terror.

One should not miss the significance of this truly remarkable passage in Amos. Here the prophet views God's rule and dominion as extending to the outermost reaches of creation. No segment of the universe—Sheol, the heavens, the high mountain, the depths of the sea, or the far country—is beyond the pale of His control. These words of Amos are all the more significant when they are studied against the background of Canaanite and Babylonian mythology, replete with its stories of conflict and struggle between the gods who represent the hosts of heaven, the sea, the storm, the mountain, and Sheol (death). In Amos' universe God's will is supreme; there is no conflict, which is tantamount to saying there is no mythology. Here the sea, the heavens, the mountain, and Sheol are completely de-personalized; they are merely the places where God carries out His search for the fugitives of Israel. Even the sea-serpent, a figure prominent in ancient mythology, is nothing more than an agent of God's destruction. That this should have been stated so clearly so early in the history of prophecy is truly remarkable.

The Third Nature Hymn (9:5-6)

This is the last of the hymns praising God for the wonders of His creation (cf. 4:13; 5:8-9). Verse 5 is an almost exact parallel to 8:8; and the latter part of verse 6 is a repetition of 5:8b. This hymn depicts God as having His dwelling place in the heavens, with His vault, or firmament, resting upon the earth. From His abode in the heavens He touches the earth and it melts (cf. Mic. 1:3-4). The earth rises and falls like the waters of the Nile, an obvious reference to an upheaval caused by an earthquake (cf. 8:8). Verse 6b affirms God's control over the rainfall. The Canaanites regarded Baal as the god of the storm and the giver of rain, but the prophet denies this claim. The one who calls for the waters of the sea and pours them out upon the surface of the earth is the Lord.

The Destruction of the Sinful Kingdom (9:7-10)

In verse 7 there is a series of questions each of which demands an affirmative answer. Israel's relationship to the Lord is the same as that of the Ethiopians. The Lord brought up Israel from the land of Egypt; but He also brought the Philistines from Caphtor and the Syrians from Kir. Caphtor has been identified with the island of Crete, whereas the location of Kir is uncertain (cf. 1:5). This verse constitutes a tacit denial that Israel stands in any special or privileged relationship to God.

Students of the Old Testament have been quick to note the universal implications of verse 7. Lods in *The Prophets and the Rise of Judaism* has interpreted this to mean that "the God of Amos is no longer the particular god of one nation: he is the supremely just judge and the protector of all nations." Cripps calls this verse "the high-water mark of inspiration" in the Book of Amos. He compares Amos' teaching to that of Jesus, in that both conceived of the love of God as transcending the bounds of the Hebrew nation. He even suggests that the preaching of Amos prepared the way for Jesus' proclamation of salvation to the whole world.

Snaith has interpreted this verse in an entirely different light. His view is that since Israel has rejected God, her rescue from Egypt no longer has any religious significance. The exodus from Egypt had long been considered the mightiest of the acts of God (cf. 2:10), since it involved Israel's election to be the people of God. Now, however, it is characterized as just another migration of peoples, "the sort of thing that happens when nations grow restless or need more room."

Verse 8a pronounces the death sentence upon the Northern Kingdom: "Behold, the eyes of the Lord God are upon the sinful kingdom, and I will destroy it from the surface of the ground." The word translated "destroy" is the same word that appears in 2:9, where it refers to the destruction of the Amorites. In each case

God is the subject of the verb; as He once destroyed the Amorites and gave their land to Israel, so now will He destroy the Israelites from upon the face of this land. This threat is reinforced by the statement that "the eyes of the Lord God are upon the sinful kingdom" (cf. 9:4). This means that God will not take His eyes off Israel until she is completely destroyed.

It must never be forgotten, as one reads Amos, that these threats were fulfilled. Within the lifetime of many of his listeners the Assyrians marched against Israel, conquered and destroyed Samaria, and carried her people into captivity, from whence they never returned. The evidence for this is found both in the Bible (II Kings 17:5-6) and in the Annals of Sargon II. This Assyrian ruler, who completed the siege of Samaria, wrote: "I besieged and conquered Samaria, and led away as booty 27,290 of her inhabitants. I placed over them an officer of mine and imposed upon them the tribute of the former king."

In view of the threatening nature of verse 8a, there are many scholars who would view it as the original end of the prophecies of Amos. These scholars regard the section beginning with verse 8b and continuing through verse 15 as an epilogue of hope added to the prophecies of Amos at a much later time. While it is recognized that some kind of judgment is still in view in verses 8-10, it is claimed that there is a radical difference between this judgment and that proclaimed earlier in the Book of Amos. Here only the sinners and scoffers in Israel are consumed by the fires of judgment; a distinction is made between the righteous and the sinners. This interpretation is based on verse 8b: "except that I will not utterly destroy the house of Jacob," and on the last clause in verse 9: "but no pebble shall fall upon the earth."

125

C. C. Torrey places the division after verse 10, thus assigning verses 8-10 to Amos, although he concedes that 8b and the last clause in verse 9 were later additions. Torrey's view has much to commend it, especially since verses 9 and 10 do not sound as if they belonged to an epilogue of hope. Here the Lord speaks of shaking the house of Israel among all the nations as one shakes with a sieve. The verb translated "shake" comes from a root which means "to wander," "to go about as a vagabond" (cf. Num. 32:13; Isa. 24:20; 29:9; Amos 4:8; 8:12). It describes those who wander about with no sense of direction and with no definite goal.

The last phrase in verse 9 is extremely difficult to interpret. Scholars are not even in agreement as to how it should be translated. In AV it is rendered: "yet shall not the least grain fall upon the earth." The word translated "grain" is found in only one other passage in the Old Testament, II Sameul 17:13, where Hushai counsels Absalom to pull down the walls of the city in which David takes refuge, "until there be not one small stone left there." This word obviously refers to a pebble and not to a grain of corn or wheat. RSV has, therefore, translated Amos 9b: "but no pebble shall fall upon the earth." Even this translation ignores the fact that there is no preposition before the word for earth nor does this word have the characteristic ending denoting direction toward something. Since the word for pebble has the same form in the Hebrew for both the absolute and the construct, his clause could be rendered: "but no pebble of the earth shall fall."

While it is fairly simple to point out the various alternate translations of this clause, it is extremely difficult to know how it should be interpreted. Does it mean that the dust and chaff will fall through the sieve while the good grain remains in it? Or does it mean that the grain will be sifted through, while pebbles and chaff remain in the sieve? Or is this to be interpreted as a sand-sieve rather than a grain-sieve? Much uncertainty surrounds this verse. The view tentatively adopted here is that this is a passage of doom and not of hopeGod will shake Israel as pebbles in a sieve, and not one pebble will fall through the sieve. In other words, there will be no chance of escaping from this shaking. This is consistent with the prophecies of judgment found throughout the Book of Amos. Verse 10 concludes this section by predicting that the sword will slay those who boast that evil will not overtake them (cf. 6:1, 3).

ing of Amos prepared the way for Jesus' proclamation of salvation to the whole world.

QUESTIONS

1. List specific ways in which worshipers today may be guilty of insulting God.
2. In your opinion, do Christians tend to have a false sense of security about the goodness of God? If so, what remedies would you suggest?
3. Do you agree that believers who have been forgiven still suffer for their sins (e.g. David, Jacob)? Why, or why not?
4. Is running away from our problems a way of trying to escape from God? Or are we merely trying to escape from ourselves?

13
Epilogue
of Hope

Amos 9:11-15

The Book of Amos concludes with an epilogue of hope, in which is painted a glorious picture of the golden age to come. The main question with which one has to deal here is whether these words were spoken by the prophet Amos or were appended to his prophecies at a later date.

F. C. Eiselen is representative of the scholars who defend the view that these are the words of Amos. The arguments usually given in support of this view are as follows: (1) Amos may have written these words after he returned to his home in Tekoa, which would account for the references to the Southern Kingdom and to the house of David. (2) All true prophecy must be conditional, as Jeremiah 18:7-10 expressly states; it follows, therefore, that one would not expect to find only prophecies of doom in the Book of Amos. The prophets were pessimistic when they looked at men, but optimistic when they looked at God. (3) The doctrine of a remnant, while not emphasized, is nevertheless present throughout the Book of Amos. (4) The characteristic pattern of eschatology, not only in Israel but also in other ancient Near Eastern countries, was one of world-catastrophe followed by world-renewal, or, as one writer has expressed it, "of happiness which follows judgment as naturally as day follows night." When a prophet had stood in the presence of God, his last word could never be a word of defeat.

The view presented above is rejected by a considerable number of present-day scholars. George Adam Smith is representative of those who maintain that this epilogue of hope was added to the prophecies of Amos by a later scribe. The reasons given in support of this view are as follows: (1) Up to this point the message of Amos had been one of unmitigated doom. Even in Chapter 9 the prophet declares that in the coming destruction "not one of them shall flee away, not one of them shall escape" (v. 1b). Neither Sheol, nor Carmel, nor heaven, nor the sea, nor the distant land will provide a hiding-place from the wrath of God (vv. 2-4). In verse 8a one reads the categorical statement: "Behold the eyes of the Lord God are upon the sinful kingdom, and I will destroy it from the surface of the ground." Why should this prediction of destruction for the Northern Kingdom—a prediction that was precisely fulfilled in history—be toned down in verse 8b and changed into a message of pure hope in verses 11-15? Lods declares that this appendix to the Book of Amos is "so full of consolation that if it were authentic it would reduce the daring denunciations of Amos to the proportions of a village squabble." Wellhausen expressed doubt that Amos would picture milk and honey pouring from the cup of the wrath of the Lord. (2) Verse 11 refers to the booth of David that has fallen but is about to be rebuilt "as in the days of old." The booth of David could hardly refer to anything except the house of David, that is, to the line of Davidic kings in Jerusalem. This line was not destroyed until 587 B.C., when Nebuchadnezzar captured Jerusalem. This verse speaks of the destruction as having already taken place, so it must have been written

129

after 587 B.C. Since it speaks further of the imminent restoration of the line of David, it probably belongs to those prophecies of hope that are dated near the end of the Babylonian exile, or shortly after the return of the Jews to Jerusalem. (3) The style and vocabulary of this passage show a greater affinity to the exilic or post-exilic period than to the time of Amos. Harper cites a total of twelve words and phrases that were in common usage in the exilic period but not in the time of Amos. (4) One of the strongest reasons for denying this passage to Amos is that it omits the ethical element in its protrayal of the ideal age to come. The kind of day it predicts is precisely the kind of day the men of Israel were looking for (cf. 5:18)—a day of political restoration, of military conquests, of wine dripping from the mountains, and of fertility in the grain fields and vineyards. George Adam Smith exclaims, "Imagine Amos predicting a future like that!" What he had hoped to see was not this, but justice rolling down like waters and righteousness as a mighty stream. There is no indication in this passage that the people are being restored because they have repented and turned from their wicked ways. The absence of any ethical demands makes it difficult to believe that these are the words of Amos. (4) It is a well-known fact that it was contrary to Jewish custom to conclude a book of Scripture with words of doom. At the end of II Chronicles, for example, Chapter 36 originally ended with verse 21. However, since this was a verse of doom, the first three verses of Ezra were borrowed and added to Chronicles in order to eliminate the sad ending. Elsewhere in the Hebrew Bible, in the Books of Isaiah, Lamentations, Ecclesiastes, and Malachi, which end in words of doom, an artificial device has been employed to offset this: the next to the last verse has been repeated after the last verse in order to give each of these books a happy ending. This enables one to understand why an epilogue of hope would have been added to Amos' prophecies of doom.

Two things need to be said regarding the view just stated. The first is that to hold this view in no way detracts from the stature of Amos as one of the greatest personalities in Biblical literature, an inspired prophet of the Lord who proclaimed the word of the Lord without fear or favor. The second statement is that even if one adopts a late date for this epilogue of hope, it must not be regarded as uninspired literature which has in some way become attached to an inspired book. An understanding of the way in which the prophetic books were collected and edited should preclude such a restricted view of inspiration. This, too, is an inspired word of the Lord. It was a correct impulse that led later generations to see that a remnant would be preserved and that restoration would follow judgment.

George Adam Smith, who places these verses later than Amos, nevertheless recognizes their significance and their beauty. He describes this closing oracle as "a pleasant piece of music, as if the birds had come out after the thunderstorm, and the wet hills were glistening in the sun." The passage describes a time when the fortunes of Israel will be changed (v. 14). There will be a return to national splendor under the re-established dynasty of David (vv. 11-12). Verse 13 describes such bounty and prosperity that the reaper and the plowman will always be getting in each other's way. The reaper will still be harvesting the old crop when it is time for the plowman to prepare the soil for the new crop. It will be as if the hills and mountains were flowing with sweet wine. This restoration will be permanent, for the Lord declares, "I will plant them upon their land, and they shall never again be plucked up out of the and which I have given them" (v. 15). Regarding this happy ending, Snaith has written: "And so we come to the end of Amos. Please God there shall be a 'happy ending' in the presence of God."

QUESTIONS

1. When, do you believe, the promise of an abundant life for the family of Jacob was or will be fulfilled?
2. What do these promises tell us of the goodness of God?
3. Would you say that these are literal or figurative promises?

Bibliography

The following bibliography is furnished for those who wish to pursue the study of Amos in greater depth.

Cripps, Richard S., *A Critical and Exegetical Commentary on the Book of Amos*. Rev. ed. London: S.P.C.K., 1955.

Edghill, Ernest Arthur, *The Book of Amos* ("Westminster Commentaries"). Second ed. London: Methuen and Co., Ltd., 1926.

Eiselen, Frederick Carl, *The Minor Prophets*. New York: Eaton and Mains, 1907.

Fosbroke, Hughell E. W., and Lovett, Sidney, "The Book of Amos," *The Interpreter's Bible,* Vol. VI, pp. 763-853. New York: Abingdon Press, 1956.

Harper, William R., *A Critical and Exegetical Commentary on Amos and Hosea* ("International Critical Commentary"). New York: Charles Scribner's Sons, 1910.

Honeycutt, Roy L., *Amos and His Message*. Nashville: Broadman Press, 1963.

Lehrman, S. M., "Amos," *The Twelve Prophets* ("The Soncino Books of the Bible"). Edited by A. Cohen. Bournemouth: The Soncino Press, 1948.

Lüthi, Walter, *In the Time of the Earthquake*. Trans. by F. L. M. Haire and Ian Henderson. London: Hodder and Stoughton, 1940.

Marsh, John, *Amos and Micah* ("Torch Bible Commentaries"). London: S.C.M. Press, 1959.

McFadyen, John Edgar, *A Cry for Justice: A Study in Amos*. Edited by John Adams. ("Short Course Series.") Edinburgh: T. and T. Clark, 1912.

Robinson, H. Wheeler, "Amos," *The Abingdon Bible Commentary*. Edited by Frederick C. Eiselen, Edwin Lewis and David G. Downey. New York: Abingdon

Press, 1929.

Smith, George Adam, *The Twelve Prophets*. Rev. ed.
New York: Harper and Brothers, 1940. Vol. I.

Snaith, Norman H., *Amos, Hosea, and Micah* ("Epworth
Preacher's Commentaries"). London: Epworth Press,
1956.

Watts, John D. W., *Vision and Prophecy in Amos*. Lei-
den: E. J. Brill, 1958.